Getting The Facts

A Fieldwork Guide
for Evaluators
and Policy Analysts

Jerome T. Murphy

HARVARD UNIVERSITY

Goodyear Publishing Company, Inc.
Santa Monica, California 90401

To Susan and Jerry

Library of Congress Cataloging in Publication Data

Murphy, Jerome T
    Getting the facts, a fieldwork guide for
    evaluators and policy analysts.

    Bibliography: p.
    Includes index.
    1. Social sciences—Field work. 1. Title.
H61.M86   300'.28   79-20989
ISBN 0-8302-3383-0

Printed in the United States of America

Contents

Preface

Although I didn't know it at the time, the seed for this book was planted in 1967 on the island of Majuro in the Trust Territory of the Pacific Islands—the first stop of a congressional subcommittee examining the U.S. administration of the islands. I made the trip to "get the facts" for the Department of Health, Education, and Welfare. As a former math teacher, untrained observer, and someone who wasn't even sure what "methodology" meant, I drew on interviews, observations, documents, and common sense to collect my data and write my first field-based evaluation. I would like to thank Sam Halperin, Ralph Huitt, and Wilbur Cohen, my bosses at HEW, for making the trip possible, and Hugh Carey, then Chairman of the House Subcommittee, for authorizing my travel with the legislative group. They would be shocked to know that a wonderful congressional junket led to this book on methodology.

Upon my return, I circulated my report within the executive branch. Harold Howe, then U.S. Commissioner of Education, thought my portrayal of administrative problems was good and deserved wide circulation; my description of the islands brought back memories of his sailor days in Micronesia. A friend on the staff of the National Security Council thought the report was worthless and deserved to be buried—it contained no numbers, no hard evidence. Since I agreed, of course, with Howe's assessment, I was struck by my friend's narrow conception of what constituted valid data. The story of abuse and neglect could not have been accurately told by using the available statistics. My thanks to "Doc" Howe and my unnamed friend for stimulating my thinking about how we know what we know and about how little we sometimes know when we think we know a lot.

Four years later, in 1971, I began to write my doctoral dissertation on how a government program was implemented. To do the job, I needed to get close to the program, to understand it firsthand, so once again I turned to interviewing, observation, and document analysis. Some statistical data were available but they were either misleading or missed the important points. Like a good graduate student, I turned to the methodological literature in my field (political science) for help. With the exception of a book on interviewing that I didn't fully appreciate at the time, there was little to be found on fieldwork methodology. So I followed my doctoral advisor's suggestion to follow my nose. I did, and learned a lot, but always felt a bit uncomfortable for not knowing more. My thanks to David Cohen for sharing his experiences with me, not to mention his good advice about noses.

The idea was there, but what brought things together was my involvement with the Eagleton Institute of Politics at Rutgers University. Under the direction of Alan Rosenthal, Eagleton had been collaborating with state legislatures since 1966, helping with the organization and operations of legislative institutions. By 1974, when I joined the endeavor, Eagleton was focusing on the oversight function of the legislature, with a grant for a project on Education Program Review (EPR) which was funded by the Ford Foundation. I worked with Institute personnel, orienting and training legislators and their professional staffs in the review and evaluation of government programs. In our efforts with legislatures in Connecticut, Florida, Louisiana, and Wisconsin, we discovered that there was a great need for written materials to guide legislative staff, and we concluded that an important product would be a publication to provide such guidance.

From that conclusion came a paper, a longer paper, and a still longer paper, which were used in Eagleton's projects and which withstood the scrutiny of legislative staff—one of the groups I had in mind as an audience for this volume. I'd like to thank Eagleton and the Ford Foundation for their support, and I hope that this work meets their purposes in state legislatures throughout the nation. In particular, I'd like to acknowledge the substantial assistance of Fred Butler, Ralph Craft, Don Weatherspoon, and especially Carl Van Horn and Alan Rosenthal—Eagleton's cadre on legislatures. Thanks also go to the legislative staffers—serving on audit or evaluation agencies, fiscal committees, and education and other standing committees—who are doing oversight and producing evaluations. Most of the examples in the text are taken from their work.

While consulting for Eagleton in the Spring of 1976, and also teaching at the Harvard Graduate School of Education, I attended a seminar, chaired by Elliot Eisner, on the virtues of qualitative evaluation. Taken by his presentation, and concerned that methodology at Harvard meant *quantitative* methodology almost exclusively, I decided to take Eisner up on his kind offer to send a course syllabus to anyone who asked. It was through his reading list, and my growing explorations into fieldwork methodology, that I began to discover the impressive methodological literature in sociology, anthropology, journalism, law, psychology, history and art and literary criticism. Indeed, the literature goes back as far as ancient times—more than 2000 years ago, Thucydides carefully followed some of the same procedures for corroborating and cross-checking. As far as I can tell, this material is still not well known to most political scientists. My thanks to Elliot Eisner and to those many fine scholars who have plowed this field with care and wisdom for many years before me. I hope I've done them justice in adapting their ideas to the evaluation of government programs.

In the spring of 1977, I taught my first fieldwork course at Harvard. My thanks to my students for their constructive criticisms

[ix]

of my thinking and particularly to my teaching assistant, Jo-Anne Lema, who helped pull together the literature that formed the basis for the course and for much of this book. Thanks also go to Derek Bok, President of Harvard University, for a small grant to develop the course material.

With the course behind me, and with support from the Eagleton Institute and the Spencer Foundation, I got serious about turning my scrawlings into a book. In this process, a number of friends and colleagues provided invaluable suggestions, criticisms, and encouragement, and shared with me their fieldwork experiences. I would like to thank Rick Apling, Chris Argyris, By Barnes, Tony Bryk, Alan Doyle, Dick Elmore, Eleanor Farrar, Jim Levine, Mark Murphy, Rick Moore, John Pittenger, Ellen Quackenbush, Ursula Wagener, Betsy Weaver, and Carol Weiss. I especially would like to thank Patricia Graham, Tom Hickey, and Milbrey McLaughlin for their careful reading of the entire manuscript and their wise advice. Thanks also go to Arnold Meltsner and particularly Mark Moore, the editors of Goodyear's policy analysis series, for their enthusiasm and valuable suggestions. Most of all I'd like to express my gratitude to Nancy Anderson, Jack De Sanctis, Susan Johnson, and Richard Winefield for working over the manuscript with the intelligence and care they'd bring to their own.

Throughout this project I've had the good fortune to have excellent secretarial assistance. For the typing of multiple drafts and the gentle prodding, thanks go to Virginia Kosmos, Dorothy Linick, Darcy Marshall, Careyleah McCloud, Susan Smith, and particularly Gail Johnston.

Finally, I'd like to express my love and thanks to my wife, Susan, for her superb suggestions on ways to improve the manuscript, and for putting up with my preoccupation with fieldwork while neglecting my housework and familywork. Believe it or not, I'm finished.

JEROME T. MURPHY

Concord, Mass.
May 1979

Introduction

POLICYMAKERS NEED FACTS. To change a government program or to defend it, they need to know whether the program is working, how well it is working, and how it can be improved. To get the facts, they dispatch staffers with simple instructions: "Find out what's going on," they say, "and report back quickly."

Responding adequately to such an assignment is hardly a simple task. Stiff intellectual, personal, and ethical challenges confront those who try to gather facts about the operations of a government program while facing a tight deadline and working in a charged political environment. Deciding where to look for answers, what facts to emphasize, and what interpretations to assign can be major problems. Another problem is coping with officials who are reluctant to candidly describe the workings of their programs, who unintentionally misreport past events, or who have different perceptions of the same occurrences. Equally vexing problems include dealing with your own biases and those of the officials who dispatched you, asking your questions without prejudicing the answers, and distinguishing a fact from a rumor or surmise. More intimate problems concern proper personal relationships with "sources" of information within the program and the reporting of critical findings about program officials you've grown to know and like.

How you approach and resolve such problems will substantially affect the quality of the evaluation that is ultimately produced (to say nothing of your peace of mind). Many of these problems don't have definitive solutions. But you do have an opportunity to think about them in advance, and to capitalize on the knowledge and experience of evaluators and scholars who have struggled with the problem of getting and intepreting the facts. Hence this book, which attempts to synthesize and codify developing professional practices.

This text is an introduction to the evaluation of government programs through fieldwork methods. By evaluation I mean the systematic collection, analysis, and presentation of information about the operation and impact of a government-sponsored program. This might include descriptive data on how a program operates as well as on how effective it is in meeting its goals. By fieldwork methods, I mean those data collection techniques (intensive interviewing, transient observation, and document analysis) that force evaluators out of their offices and into the field to find out what's happening, how, and why. These methods allow analysts to learn about the program in context, from the points of view of those connected with it. The goal is to get a firsthand understanding of the program at work so it can be improved. The product often includes a case study on each site visited.

This is a "how to" book that offers practical suggestions on techniques and procedures. But I've also examined the difficulties of collecting valid information and the reasons certain approaches are important. Among questions considered are: Why do subjects provide inaccurate information? Why use multiple methods to collect data on the same point? Why share your drafts with the agency being evaluated? I've also tried to present the logic of the field evaluation, and to describe what it feels like to do one and to write the report. The work can be exhausting and frustrating, but it can also be enormous fun as you track down clues, follow up leads, and wrestle a problem to the ground.

[4]

This book is aimed at the growing number of students, evaluators, policy analysts, planners, applied researchers and practitioners who are turning to fieldwork techniques to do short-term assessments of government programs. It is also designed to be helpful to government and foundation officers who might sponsor such work, to policymakers and critics who want to know how to judge a good report, and to the general public who want to learn more about getting the facts. The text can be used in workshops and courses on evaluation and policy analysis, and can be easily understood by those not participating in any formal training program.

In short, the book is intended to help the novice fieldworker dig better, cope with the problems of bias and error, avoid over-simplifying complicated issues, and treat public programs and officials fairly. It is meant as a road map—far from perfectly charted—across complex terrain.

Some Background

Since the mid-sixties, the interest in evaluating government programs has increased dramatically. At the federal level, $146 million was spent on nondefense program evaluation in 1974, up 500 percent from 1969. And in 1977, 2100 "full-time equivalents" worked in the federal government on program evaluation.[1] At the state level, executive agencies and legislative bodies are more involved with program evaluation and oversight than ever before. To help evaluators, new professional journals on evaluation and newsletters aimed at practitioners have recently been established.[2] All this interest reflects the flood of social legislation passed during the sixties and early seventies. Specific legislative provisions require evaluation and there is increasing concern about accountability and efficiency in government programs. In all likelihood, the demand for systematic information about government programs will continue to grow.

To date, most of the disciplined work in evaluation has relied on rigorous statistical methods to determine whether programs produce their intended effects. Hard-working, sophisticated, quantitative methodologists have developed imaginative research designs, reliable sampling procedures, sophisticated measures of outcomes, and codified procedures for analyzing data. Much of this work has been quite valuable in accurately depicting program outcomes. Nonetheless, this approach has severe limits, thus leading to this text on a different, *complementary* approach to assessing government programs. Statistical outcome analysis may be powerful, but there are many situations where it cannot be easily applied, or where the data produced are inappropriate or inadequate for answering the most important evaluation questions.

For example, outcome studies are inappropriate when host agencies simply absorb new resources instead of putting a new program into practice. For instance, funds from Title I of the Elementary and Secondary Education Act (ESEA), were to be spent on special compensatory programs for disadvantaged children. But initially the money often supplemented the regular program budgets for all children.[3] In such cases, what happened and why? Are the programs in compliance with the law? What are the obstacles to improved practice? The statistical analyses of outcome data can't answer these questions.

Innovative, exploratory programs also are inadequately evaluated by conventional outcome studies. These programs are characterized by shifting goals, changing program activities, and wide variations from site to site. Priorities and content are determined as staff learn from experience, participants enter and leave the program, and the program adapts to its organizational, political, and social environment. This evolutionary process is not indicative of a poorly implemented program—it is the appropriate way to implement complex, exploratory programs.[4] Thus, it is a mistake to measure only a few outcomes as if the program and its goals were uniform, well-defined and unchanged from the original conceptions. Documenting the evolution and changing impact of such a program provides more useful information.

[6]

Outcome studies are also weak in evaluating programs with multiple, broad purposes. How can you fairly represent the diverse program aims? For example, ESEA Title I was viewed by different people as serving diverse purposes—breaking the federal aid barrier, raising schoolchildren's achievement, helping to pacify the ghettos, assisting private school children, providing fiscal relief to school districts, and reducing poverty.[5] Strict indicators such as test scores show only a small portion of the impact of such a program. What's more, since large-scale government interventions like Title I have unanticipated consequences that might be as important, or more important, than the intended outcomes, it is desirable to resist the straightjacket of a set of quantitative indicators specified in advance. We want to see what the program actually produces in a variety of areas.[6]

Even when statistical analyses of outcomes adequately measure goal achievement, such information by itself is often relatively unimportant to a policymaker. After all, what does a legislator or program manager do with information showing that a program has not raised test scores? Terminate the program? Demand improvement? The reality of politics and management is that go/no-go decisions are seldom made as a result of single evaluations. Therefore, what's needed is information intelligible to the layperson that will help make programs run better. To make sensible recommendations for improvement, you need to understand how people perceive the program, and how it operates and why.[7]

These criticisms certainly are not intended to imply that statistical studies are useless or that statistical data shouldn't be used as evidence in a field study. Nor are they meant as a Fuller Brush pitch for fieldwork methods. The approach is labor-intensive, expensive and hard to do well, and the reliance on "soft" data invites charges of bias and impressionism. Rather, this discussion provides a rationale for adopting a more eclectic, but equally disciplined, way of gathering information about the operations and effects of a given program. There is valid information in the world beyond that contained in outcome statistics, and there are rigorous procedures for collecting, verifying, and presenting fieldwork data.

[7]

What Follows

Faced with this broad demand for evaluations and the limits of conventional approaches, it is not surprising that there is an increasing demand for analysts who are both interested in evaluating government programs and familiar with fieldwork techniques. However, good training material is not available for these professionals who must do short-term evaluations containing more than summary judgments about program outcomes.[8] What follows is meant to respond to that need.

Once a program has been selected for evaluation and you've been assigned to do the work, you need to decide on the basic questions to be explored. Chapter 1 deals with these, the ideas that shape the direction of an evaluation. The next steps are to get a preliminary grasp of the program, choose sites for data collection, and arrange to get into—and stay in—the sites. These are covered in Chapter 2.

The next three chapters deal with the actual collection of data. Your aims are to choose the most appropriate method and to avoid bias and error. Chapter 3 discusses the major sources of bias and error and presents some general safeguards against them. Chapter 4 covers the ins and outs of intensive interviewing as the primary method of data collection. Chapter 5 explores two crucial supplementary methods—transient observation and document analysis.

As you collect information, you begin analyzing it, trying to make sense out of a chaotic accumulation. This process, starting in the field, goes into high gear when you return to your office to organize your thoughts on paper. Chapter 6 offers some guidance on analyzing and writing, and for good measure includes some practical suggestions about what to do when you get stuck. In the end, is your analysis any good? Chapter 7 focuses on the substance of the most important sections—conclusions and recommendations—and presents standards for judging the quality of the final report.

As you read through the text, you may feel at times the way I do after a tennis lesson or two. Bombarded with advice on how to cock my wrist, bend my knees, point my toes, and lean forward, I end up paralyzed. There are so many things to remember and do that I hardly do anything at all. And what happened to the fun?

But learning to do fieldwork is different from the way I've been taught tennis. There is no one best way, there are few unconditional rules, and you need not fall asleep every night worrying about "all those bad habits" ruining your game. You certainly need not memorize everything suggested and coordinate it all perfectly. Rather, you learn to do fieldwork mainly by doing it—by making your own mistakes and developing strokes that work for you, preferably under the guidance of a seasoned evaluator. For the novice, learning comes from imitation and feedback, but mostly from experience.

In all, you don't just meander into the field to casually collect "the facts" and return to write the definitive report. There are booby traps planted all along the path. But there are also systematic ways to identify and defuse them. A good analyst is aware of the problems, insists on high quality data, and uses multiple methods to check out conflicting evidence. He also recognizes that his objective is a convincing argument based on persuasive evidence, not perfect proof based on all the facts.

1

The Evaluation
Questions

T HE QUESTIONS THAT are most appropriately studied with fieldwork methods are those concerning *program operations* (How does the program work? What really happened?), and *program improvement* (What explains problems? Are there better alternatives?). These are the areas emphasized in this book. In addition, fieldwork methods are important in examining some *goal-related results* (Is the program complying with the law? Is it meeting its goals?). All three categories are discussed in detail below. The study of program compliance as well as the hows and whys of program operations is often referred to as the study of policy implementation.[1]

Keep in mind throughout that, while the questions seem distinct, in fact they overlap and are often posed simultaneously. Virtually all at once, you might be examining goals, exploring program operations, gauging success, uncovering shortcomings, speculating about their reasons, and perhaps even testing out tentative recommendations.

I. GOAL-RELATED RESULTS

In many evaluations, a primary concern is whether a program is meeting its goals. Policymakers state this question in several different ways: Is the program effective? Is it working? Is it in compliance with the law? Do the results square with intent? Is the program a success?

Fieldwork techniques are particularly useful in answering compliance-oriented questions (Does the program follow regulations and guidelines? Does the program serve the "right" children?) Fieldwork techniques are also useful in studying goal conformity in areas not amenable to conventional statistical analysis (improvement in school climate, relevance of a program to children), in contrast to studies of more remote outcomes (Did the program raise the children's test scores?).

The study of goal-related results is often an important part of a field evaluation, providing a valuable supplement to data on program operations and other program results. Such study requires an idea of program goals, standards of comparison to measure success in achieving them, and specific indicators to evidence the level of goal achievement.

Program Goals

You obviously need to know a program's goals in order to say whether it's producing the results intended. A general conception of goals also helps guide the study of program operations, discussed later. The question is how do you find out what they are?

Analysts usually attempt to derive program goals by exploring the original legislative intent. You can do this by reading documents (for example, the law, legislative records, debates), and by talking with officials familiar with the legislative history (for example, key legislators, legislative staff, budget analysts, program administrators). You can also consult with those outside government who have an interest or stake in the program's operation (for example, beneficiaries, lobbyists, dissatisfied groups, advocacy groups).

The deeper you get, the murkier things often become. The written record (if any) will normally show that while some provisions of the law were debated, others were not. Generalities were discussed but not defined. Specific statements of intent were later contradicted, sometimes by the same person. Different individuals and groups will have different conceptions of the program's intent, often in conflict with the views of the central agency administering the program. Indeed, a foray into legislative history can heighten your confusion about the "real" legislative purpose.

There are several reasons for this conflict and confusion. First, legislators often make deliberately vague statements of intent to try to build a coalition behind a bill; conflicting interests each believe the legislation will serve their priorities once it is implemented. Not surprisingly, you find this conflict when you inquire about program goals. Second, those responsible for passing laws are often themselves not sure of the goals. They recognize a problem (for example, the inadequate education of poor children, whatever "inadequate" means), and believe it needs to be solved. But they do not know exactly how, nor do they know what a program's impact might be (or should be), except in general. If program advocates are this vague, resist the temptation to invent clear goals that would permit a neat, uncomplicated evaluation. And be wary of statements of "*the* central goals" offered by a particular individual or group.

Instead of using goals derived from legislative history, it may be preferable to look at the program in light of its current goals, developed through experience in implementing the program. This often-overlooked alternative is particularly sensible for vaguely defined programs marked by changing goals and poorly understood processes. But here, also, you will probably find conflict.

In part because of the conflicts, you can expect to find a variety of program purposes. Further complicating your work is that programs also facilitate *personal* goals (a new job, a promotion, money to travel); *organizational* goals (maintenance and expansion of an agency); *political* goals (the redistribution of power and resources); and *symbolic* goals (a failing poverty program might be continued because it expresses government commitment to helping the poor). "Program goals" mean different things to different people and, for some, success will have little to do with achievement of any defined substantive goals.

With the various goals identified, how do you measure goal-related results? Ideally, you should collect data associated with all the identified goals. This would make the evaluation responsive to its various audiences and perhaps gain their support for implementing recommendations. Practically speaking, however, the difficulty of collecting data on some goals and your tight deadline will force a limit. So do as much as you can, aiming for enough breadth to prevent the final report from being dismissed for overlooking important results or for not including those goals that the evaluation's sponsors believe are crucial (both for the program and politically). Whatever goals you end up examining, you should recognize that no abridged list will satisfy everyone.[2]

Standards of Comparison

The next step is to think about standards of comparison, the yardsticks that indicate the level of progress toward goal achievement, and provide the basis for making statements about program success. A numerical example graphically illustrates both how standards vary and how determining "success" is a lot more complicated than it first appears. Suppose a state program's goal was to substantially increase the number of handicapped children served by the local schools. Two years later the percentage of handicapped children served had tripled from twenty to sixty percent of the 10,000 handicapped children in the state. This seems a substantial increase. But is the program "a success?"

The answer depends on your yardstick. Applying a commonly used standard, *preprogram conditions*, the program is a success because many more students are being served now than before the state's intervention.

Other standards include a *planned target*, and *the hopes and expectations* of key individuals. If the state department of education had set a two-year target of quadrupling the number of handicapped children served, the program could be declared a failure. If legislators had hoped that all handicapped children would be served after two years, it also could be judged a failure. Alternatively, you could conclude that these standards were unfair. Many have drawn such a conclusion, for instance, about the expectation that the War on Poverty would eliminate poverty in ten years.

Another standard is *need*. Advocates for the handicapped might argue that all handicapped children need to be served. Since that didn't happen by the end of the second year, the program is not yet a full success.

A final standard lies between preprogram conditions and (often grand) expectations. Here the focus is on the feasible, a *recognized standard of excellence*. If, for example, the leading school districts in the state have tripled the number of children they serve and if respected experts think that no more can reasonably be expected, the overall program might be declared a success for reaching this level of performance.

A crucial issue on standards concerns who chooses them and who applies them. One likely possibility is to solicit the views of those paying for the evaluation. For example, key legislators or program managers might have a clear idea of what a substantial increase means to them. A second possibility is to exercise your own judgment in choosing appropriate standards. If you do so, you should be explicit in the final report about the standards you applied and the evidence used to reach your conclusions.

A third possibility is to have one or more experts compare the program with expectations, generally based on their experience or on theory. Such experts should be highly regarded by key policymakers—or of sufficient stature to command that regard through their experience or reputation—and should not have a stake in the program.

A fourth often-overlooked possibility is to ask program participants and clients (for example, teachers, hospital workers, welfare recipients) to assess program success. Through careful questioning you can determine the goals that they think are important and their standards of comparison. Of course, this alternative can lead to self-serving assessments, but the views of those closest to the program can also provide helpful insights into what's working that are often missed by other observers.

A fifth possibility is to set forth your judgments in an "if-then" form. For example, *if* the program goal is to eliminate outdated procedures in the welfare program's administration—a stated target serves as the standard—*then* the program is a failure by this standard because a computer has yet to be utilized. But *if* the results are compared with preprogram conditions, *then* the program is a success because new auditing procedures have been instituted.

A final possibility is to simply present your findings and interpretations, allowing the readers to make their own judgments about the program's relative success. These last two approaches have the advantage of sidestepping the issue of the appropriate standard of comparison, which is inevitably controversial and as a result can deflect or delay any real effort to deal with the findings and recommendations.

Depending on the standards used and on who applies them, the evaluation can reach quite different conclusions about the program's success. These possibilities should be examined when you discuss strategies for designing and conducting your evaluation. The complexity of answering the seemingly simple question, "Is the program a success?" should not be underplayed when reporting on your work.[3]

Program Indicators

With your goals and yardsticks identified, the next step is to think about indicators of goal conformity—that is, the specific evidence that will demonstrate whether the program has produced its intended effects. Ideally, each program goal is directly assessed by multiple indicators.

Sometimes these indicators are formulated before you enter the field. An example comes from a study of an education program with the goal of rearranging the relationships between the school and the work place. The analysts devised several indicators:

> *One is role change.* For employers . . . the innovation re-
> quires an expansion of roles to include instruction, the evalu-
> ation of student work, discipline, a liaison with school
> officials . . . .
>
> [*Another*] . . . *involves the location of learning.* [The in-
> novation] . . . aims to expand the location of student learning
> by the establishment of work exploration and experience
> sites, and by organizing school work around activities in
> those sites . . . . These aspects . . . would be revealed in the
> observation of student experiences, in the reports of teachers
> and employees, in self-reports by students, and in curriculum
> content.[4]

This example illustrates the usefulness of nonquantitative indicators where numerical scales don't exist. It also shows the inventiveness of analysts dealing with the difficult task of identifying
indicators before entering the field.

Sometimes, however, significant indicators aren't formulated
until *after* you enter the field and see what's happening. An
example comes from a Connecticut evaluation of the state's compensatory education program. According to the law, the program's
goal was to serve "children restricted by economic, social, or
environmental disadvantage," but these terms were not defined.

To present compliance data, the analysts "describe the criteria actually used and make some judgments as to whether they fit what the state seems to want."[5]

Another example of indicators devised in the field comes from a Connecticut evaluation of programs for handicapped children:

> The . . . staff originally intended to use criteria developed in previous research projects to assess programs . . . . Unfortunately a review of the professional literature and current research revealed that such criteria do not exist . . . . In the absence of specific criteria . . . the criteria used . . . consisted solely of what was expected by care providers and consumers, or what was reported in terms of individual progress in a particular placement situation.[6]

This also illustrates the need for inventiveness, due to a typical problem: the absence of readily-available indicators for measuring goal-related results.[7]

Concluding Caution

Remember that your time is limited. The very process of defining goals, standards, and indicators could easily consume the time available for the entire evaluation. Delving into legislative history, puzzling over the meaning of success, and devising appropriate measures of results can be fascinating, with additional twists and turns always ready to be explored. However, limits must be established. Otherwise you'll have no time to collect the data, and little opportunity to learn what you inevitably will learn as you get into the field.

II. PROGRAM OPERATIONS

As argued in the Introduction, program evaluation is ultimately concerned with making things better, and you need to know how things are actually working to make reasonable suggestions for improvement. As also argued, some programs are especially appropriate candidates for asking what happened, how, and why—innovative projects, new programs not fully operational, and broadly-aimed programs with important unanticipated consequences.

This suggests examining program inputs, operations and impact, and the process of implementation over time. The basic evaluation questions become: What is the nature of the program and how does it work in practice? How have the program and its goals changed and developed? What forces have shaped its evolution? What impact has it had, unintended as well as intended? What is the significance of what has happened? How well has the program been implemented?

As these questions suggest, the study of program operations is usually more exploratory than the study of goal-related results. Analysts often discover the important issues (and how to gather data on them) *after* going into the field and sniffing around to find out what's happening. This exploration may lead to detours and blind alleys, but initially you follow the program where it takes you, even down unexpected, uncharted paths. Like explorers, analysts of program operations know the general direction in which they are moving, but often make significant discoveries along the way.

Your evaluation will reflect this exploration. Your report will usually rely heavily on descriptive data presented in narrative form, the story of the program's development. Your account will include a generous sprinkling of quotes from reports, program participants, and knowledgeable observers. It will put in context the things that have happened and changed because of the government funding. At its best, it can give policymakers an accurate feel for the program in action, and relevant information to act on.

Relevant Data

Not all the information available is relevant and worth interpreting, of course. The data that analysts do collect should be largely determined by the evaluation sponsors' general conception of what is relevant. This means asking sponsors about their general concerns, about what they see as the problems and issues to be investigated.

A concern might take the form of a puzzling inconsistency (for example, a program provides millions of dollars for job training and placement, yet program graduates don't remain employed). Another concern might involve a dilemma about next steps (for example, different responses to a faltering economy could produce either inflation or unemployment). Other concerns might grow out of undesirable consequences (for example, a pollution control program that seems to have resulted in higher prices). Still other concerns might involve specific program issues or matters of dispute (for example, people disagree as to whether a hospital program adequately serves the poor). Or, evaluation sponsors may be concerned because of confusion about the program, a break in tradition, or a redistribution of power. If feasible, you might examine the nature of the concern, the reasons for it, its impact, and ways to improve things. Sponsor concerns, then, help organize and delimit the search for relevant data.[8]

The information that analysts collect is also determined by assumptions, often subconscious, about what is important and what is trivial. During the last decade or so, social scientists have taken various sets of assumptions about the way government works and packaged them into what they call conceptual frameworks or models.[9] These different sets of assumptions focus on different factors—individual or group behavior, organizational processes (routines and standard procedures), couplings between organizational units, and decision-making processes. Different models provide different lenses for viewing a program, and these lenses influence what data are collected and reported. That is, different analysts with different lenses will tell partially different stories about the same program.

This is not the place to explore the details of various models, but rather to point out the importance of the assumptions you bring to the evaluation. Try to be aware of them, and rely on common sense and experience in choosing important program dimensions to analyze.

Five Dimensions

The various kinds of data required will, of course, have different emphases depending on the program and your concerns. Broadly speaking, however, policymakers are usually interested in data along the following five dimensions.

First, evidence on the program's current *organizational and political setting* will put the discussion of the specific program and its operation into a broader context. It will also identify the various environmental constraints and forces affecting the program's delivery. Each agency has its own history, traditions, habits, accepted programs, and procedures. These attributes develop over time as a result of the political environment, the training, experiences and expectations of the staff, the structure of the organization and its systems of rewards and punishments, and the agency's constituencies. The setting that results from this mix of influences will probably affect the delivery of the program being evaluated. Consequently, important facts about the organizational and political setting should be included in the report.

A legislative evaluation of school accountability in Florida highlights the influence of a changing program environment:

> The single most significant event in the recent history of education in Florida is the statewide teachers' strike of 1968. The strike serves as a reference point, a watershed in time, around which can be described the many changes that have recently taken place in education and which are still occurring. The changing attitudes of the public toward schools and

[23]

teachers, the relationship between the education community
and the Legislature, and the changing role of the Department
of Education—all can be discussed in terms of what happened in 1968.[10]

Second, evidence on *essential program features*, those characteristics that show how the program works, will tell the story of its
operation and delivery. This evidence might include basic statistics on who participates in the program, who runs it and who
actually benefits—how, when, and where. It might include program costs, appropriations and available resources. It might include details on current organizational structures, practices and
procedures, including how decisions are made and carried out. It
might report on program priorities and needs, as well as on consequences and utilization. It might also include an analysis of the
way the state regulates, monitors, audits, and evaluates local
projects, plus data on the character of intergovernmental relations.
Finally, the report might focus on the interrelationships among all
these factors and the differences from site to site.

An evaluation of Connecticut special education illustrates a
discussion of program delivery:

> When an agency, such as the Department of Children and
> Youth Services, assumes the guardianship of a child, the
> agency can request an out-placement [i.e., placing the child
> in a PF—private facility] and may also designate a PF where
> the child is to be placed. The LEA [local education agency]
> in such cases is almost stripped of its capacity to follow
> established out-placement procedures. Moreover, the LEA is
> assessed the fees for payment of an education program in a PF
> which was chosen, not by the LEA, but by the agency. In
> these situations, the LEA's Planning and Placement Team
> appears, in effect, to be a rubber stamp.[11]

The Florida school accountability evaluation includes a discussion of program utilization:

> Up to now this report has concentrated on Department ac-
> tivities, program administration, and the intent of the Legis-
> lature's many mandates. This section will attempt to review
> who uses assessment data, for what and how. . . .[12]

Third, evidence on *key individuals and institutions* will describe
those influential in the program's passage and implementation.
These might include legislators, legislative staff, state and local
project managers, budget analysts and program specialists, a variety of state and local agencies, commissions, advisory groups and
offices, interest group representatives and lobbyists, media representatives, independent experts and consultants, research firms,
and advocacy groups. The data reported might include who they
are, what roles they have played, what they do as part of their jobs,
how they have exerted influence, how they have interacted, how
they perceive the program, and how they view themselves as well
as other key individuals and institutions and the program itself.

The Florida school accountability evaluation illustrates conflicting perceptions held by key program participants:

> This [legislative] view of what Chapter 71-197 requires con-
> trasts markedly with the opinions of the Department person-
> nel responsible for its implementation. Extensive conversa-
> tions with the associate deputy commissioner, one of those
> involved in the writing of the Senate amendments . . . indi-
> cate that the Department felt the act gave legislative en-
> dorsement to its own earlier plan. . . .[13]

The Connecticut compensatory education evaluation analyzes
the activities of key state officials:

> [The program has] five full-time regular employees respon-
> sible for about $20 million in compensatory education funds
> distributed to 165 school districts. . . .
>
> The state compensatory education staff view themselves first
> and foremost as educators, not as monitors, auditors, or

policemen. "I don't think we're seen as inspectors when we visit LEA's . . . ," commented one staffer. . . . This program orientation certainly can be defended on educational grounds, but it is not without cost. If nothing else, it reduces the amount of time available to a small staff for insuring that the letter of the law is being met.[14]

Fourth, evidence on *the program's evolution* will show how the program, its goals, its impact, its participants, and its environment have changed over time, and highlight continuing issues and problems. The report, in effect, will present a running account of what things were like before the program, what happened when the program was initiated, the developing process of implementation, and how the program has interacted with its changing political and organizational setting. The amount of attention devoted to an historical account will vary considerably, depending upon the stability of the program, the interest of the evaluation's sponsors, and its importance to an understanding of the program's character and consequences.

An evaluation of Wisconsin compensatory education illustrates a focus on the evolving state administration of a new program:

> Staffing changes . . . resulted in different program philosophies being espoused at first. The initial lack of continuity slowed program planning and development. . . . Guidelines were developed by mid-1974 and have been improved each year thereafter. A State . . . Advisory Committee has been involved in this activity although its involvement has decreased recently.[15]

Fifth, evidence will be collected on *how well* the program is operating. Just as standards are used to gauge effectiveness in meeting goals, standards can be used to gauge success in program operation. One such standard is *accepted practice*. For example, fiscal control activities in a government program could be compared with nationally-accepted procedures. If the program matched the standards, it would be a success in this phase of its operations.

A second standard is *accepted notions about the characteristics of well-implemented programs.* Practitioners and researchers contend that a program is successfully implemented when it has become part of the host institution's ongoing activities and shows signs of persistence. This normally happens, it is argued, only if both the organization and the new program adapt to the unique conditions of their marriage. In comparing a program with such a standard, develop indicators just as described earlier in comparing a program with its goals. A recent study suggests three such indicators:

> mutual modification . . .[of the existing agency and the new programs]
> emergence of new constituencies commited to the [program]
> evidence of ongoing commitment to and incorporation of the . . . [program] (i.e., budget lines, program plans, staff commitments, etc.).[16]

If the program evidenced these characteristics, you could conclude that it was "successfully" implemented.

III. PROGRAM IMPROVEMENT

If the evaluation shows that the program is not making reasonable progress toward its goals, or that it is being poorly operated, the program should either be terminated or improved. Because termination is not typically a realistic political option, I emphasize improvement. Recommendations for improvement (see Chapter 7) must be based on an understanding of *what went wrong and why.*

Ideally, an evaluation would closely examine all program problems and all the reasons for them. But the reasons for foul-ups are usually multiple and complex, and program participants are frequently reluctant to discuss them. Many problems don't lend themselves to either easy understanding or workable solutions. Because of this complexity as well as limited time and a concern with practical, short-term recommendations, you need to establish priorities. For example, it may be that low salaries and fiscal stringency are important problems for local agencies implementing a program. Though these problems deserve discussion in your report, they might not be worth much data-collection time because they probably won't be solved in the short run through state action. Perhaps the program was poorly conceived, with unsound assumptions connecting certain program elements to certain outcomes—for example, some researchers suggest that compensatory education is an unsound strategy because extra school dollars don't result in improved achievement. In such cases, exploring the reasons for failure might require detailed research on the fundamental assumptions. This type of exploration is usually done by basic researchers with adequate time and resources, not by analysts undertaking a short-term program evaluation.

Focus most of your attention on manipulable factors, those elements that really can be changed in an effort to improve the program. Such factors might include *administrative* problems, such as inadequate cost controls, substandard procedures, outmoded management techniques, inefficient allocation of manpower, weak leadership, insufficient staff training, or little opportunity for professional growth. They might be *governance* problems, such as inadequate parental involvement or domination by professionals. They might be *intergovernmental relations* problems, such as useless monitoring, nonexistent auditing, unintelligible regulations, unduly restrictive guidelines, or bureaucratic red tape. They might be *money* problems, such as underfunding or overfunding. And they might be *logistical* problems. For example, it was assumed in one state that the elderly would participate in a new recreational program, only to discover that the absence of free transportation was a major barrier.

Remember, though, that what appears to be manipulable may not be so at all. For example, useless monitoring might be explained by the state's inability to impose its will on local units. Political problems are often misperceived as managerial problems, illustrating the importance of understanding why the problems exist.

Here are several examples of problems and explanations from recent evaluations. From the Connecticut special education evaluation comes an analysis of one shortcoming:

> The financing of out-placements was another problem area. Under the present system, LEA's bear the initial cost of . . .care and do not receive reimbursement from the State until 12 to 18 months later . . .These expenses are more burdensome because they may not be anticipated; one local administrator noted that: "An out-placement . . .is something that is expected but not included in budget preparations . . .these children moving into the district needing residential treatment, means that a $16,000 budget item that no one even figured on . . .is now there . . . ."[17]

The Connecticut compensatory education evaluation provides an explanation for continued program abuses:

> . . .years of monitoring have not eliminated . . .abuses. The question is why.

> Part of the problem has to do with the size and complexity of the Hartford schools, and the resultant big-city bureaucratic buck-passing. "We just couldn't find anybody really responsible for some . . .programs there," laments one SEA official . . . .[18]

The Florida school accountability evaluation includes an explanation of administrative problems:

> The lack of progress in developing an overall management information system despite legislative requests and mandates dating back to at least 1968 can be ascribed to the difficulty of the task, to the large financial and personnel resources required for successful creation and implementation of a system and, most critical of all, to a lack of consensus between the Department and the Legislature as to what kinds of management decisions are needed and consequently what kinds of information should be brought to bear on those decisions by the system.[19]

In looking for problems and ideas for improvement, be aware of several dangers. Sometimes analysts, under pressure to formulate recommendations, identify manipulable variables not because they might lead to improvement but because they can at least lead to action; meanwhile, real explanations lie elsewhere. There is also a danger in the opposite direction. Sometimes analysts too quickly say nothing can be done, that changing variables won't change the program, and that the real problems are too complex to be manipulated.

A third danger is overlooking what went right, and why. Focusing on what's working provides good people with recognition they deserve and encourages them to do an even better job. It also helps build credibility for the evaluation—positive statements counter the argument that the evaluation team was simply out to destroy people and programs. And, most important, it identifies tested ideas that might be put into wider practice.

A fourth danger is misplacing the blame for shortcomings. Slow implementation of a complicated program might be blamed on program administrators when the real problem is unreasonable expectations on the part of policymakers or program evaluators. New programs, even those run by the best people, typically take time to get under way. Or a program might have been designated a decade ago to serve a particular group. In the meantime, the size of that group has doubled. If the program now serves half the group, it is working well by yesterday's standard, but falling short of today's need. In cases like this, the program might not need to be improved, but expanded.

Despite the difficulties and uncertainties in exploring what went wrong and why, the importance of the endeavor can hardly be overemphasized. Analysts who do not examine shortcomings, and who do not understand at least tentatively why a program worked as it did, are in a poor position to generate realistic recommendations.

2

Off and Running

A GOOD REPORT on program operations and improvement often requires in-depth data gathered through fieldwork techniques. The analyst collects extensive data at only a few sites (for example, schools, hospitals, welfare offices). How do you choose those sites? How do you arrange to get into them and stay in? These two questions are considered below. But first comes an essential preliminary activity—immersing yourself in the readily available information about the program.

I. Scouting the Scene

California Joe was a famous Indian scout in the 1850s. His job was to ride ahead of a wagon train, size up the situation, and report back to the trail boss on approaching problems and how to proceed. California Joe would read the country along the trail, watch for signs of enemy movement, and talk with trusted contacts. It was his job to know about river fords, empty waterholes, disease-infested settlements, roving bandits, and hostile Indians. With this information, wagon train leaders knew what trails to take, what settlements to avoid, what problems to expect and how to respond—all this got the weary pioneers safely to Oregon before winter set in.

In some ways, program analysts are modern-day scouts. Packing pencils instead of guns and tracking reports instead of trails, they check ahead, size up the situation, and guide the evaluation. Scouting is particularly important in the early stages of program evaluation.

The initial scouting consists mostly of reading everything available about the program being evaluated. Check legislative documents, annual reports, applications from local agencies, audit reports, internal memoranda, notes from agency meetings, program evaluations, newspaper articles, and material about similar programs in other states. In the very beginning, everything may seem equally important. But after trekking through thickets of reports and program descriptions, you will find that your trail keeps crossing certain problems and issues.

Besides heavy reading, the initial scouting also entails some preliminary interviews, often by telephone, to find out what's happening in the program and to discover who's interested in the evaluation. The logical place to start interviewing is with program administrators in the executive branch. They should have statewide information and they should know the different groups and individuals with a stake in the program. But this approach doesn't always work, as illustrated in a Connecticut evaluation of financial aid to college students.[1] The analyst's request for basic information from the Commission of Higher Education met considerable resistance; the program administrator apparently felt that his territory was being invaded. Consequently, the analyst spoke directly with the financial aid officers in Connecticut's colleges and university. Other potential sources of data might include a trusted contact in the bureaucracy, a former program administrator, a legislative staffer familiar with the program, a lobbyist, or a media person.

All this scouting, taking several days to a week, serves several purposes. First, it helps identify those individuals and groups playing key roles in the program's delivery. This information is essential if you hope to ask intelligent questions of the right people. Second, the scouting helps identify the goals and concerns of various audiences with an interest in the evaluation. Besides the sponsors of the evaluation, these might include citizens, program operators, lobbyists, media representatives, budget analysts, scholars, policy analysts, and professional evaluators.

A third purpose of scouting is to allow you to get a glimpse of the program terrain—its makeup, issues, and problems. It is possible not only to discover the crucial questions, but also to figure out what data are important and available. Fourth, scouting can provide some preliminary information about potential sites for data collection and potential problems in gaining entry. And fifth, it can help you learn the jargon of the program being evaluated—it is important to be able to crack the code, even if you don't want to reproduce it.

The scouting process, what it takes and personal reactions, is well illustrated in a note written by a novice during his first evaluation assignment:

> Well, here it is already Thursday: we started this reading and studying process last Friday, so this is the fifth work day of just that, plus some night reading. And it was only yesterday that I began to get some idea of what some of the important issues and questions might be. . . .
>
> Then there's the time not spent reading . . . talking with [the team leader] about scheduling and plans; asking him questions about something I read which didn't really fit in just yet; making phone calls and writing letters to request more information to read; making copies, etc.
>
> And now the last couple of days, I've been able to spend some time taking notes, jotting down ideas I have about what I'm reading, and even beginning to formulate some questions which are beginning to seem important.

> There's a conflict here: we want to really get into this
> stuff. . . . So it's necessary for a new person to do what I've
> done these past few days. But the rub is that there are only so
> many weeks and days to do all the interviews and writ-
> ing, . . .Already I've got a feeling that we have to get moving.
> And not going to Hartford or New Haven this week (found
> out this morning we can't see [a former program adminis-
> trator] until Wednesday) makes me a little anxious.[2]

In short, scouting yields a tentative working knowledge of the
program. It also helps identify the information needs of various
audiences and how they will probably react to the evaluation.
Having become familiar with the lay of the land, you are in a
position to select sites and to try to gain entry.

II. SELECTING SITES

Small samples, a characteristic of fieldwork, open evaluators to the
charge that the sites studied are unique, so the conclusions can't be
generalized. It is not enough to retort that generalizing from any
social science sample is now being questioned,[3] or that you sac-
rificed breadth for depth to gain a better understanding of the
program in context. You need to anticipate the criticism and take
steps to reduce it. But how? The answer depends in part upon the
purpose of the evaluation.

Most field evaluations are designed to explore a *variety* of
specific questions, issues, and hypotheses (hunches) about the
nature of the program and its impact. The points emphasized in the
final report are largely figured out in the process of doing these
exploratory evaluations. Some evaluations, however, are designed to demonstrate the plausibility of a specific hypothesis. The
chief focus is determined before doing these *hypothesis-guided*
evaluations. These two types of program evaluation can have
different criteria for site selection, which are examined in this
section. Much of the criticism of evaluations that rely on small

samples can be averted by careful attention to these criteria in selecting your sites. Credibility can also be enhanced by comparing your results with those of other studies and by candidly discussing the limits of your sample in your final report.[4]

Exploratory Evaluations

One way to minimize criticism of a small sample when conducting an exploratory evaluation is to select sites that vary widely along several dimensions. This *diversity strategy* helps "map the space," and protects against the argument that the findings apply only to a few sites with the same basic character, facing the same kinds of problems. For example, when the Florida House Education Committee staff decided to conduct interviews in ten of the state's sixty-seven school districts, care was taken to include districts that varied in urban/rural character and in geographical location.[5] Other possible dimensions include agency size, budget, percentage of budget from the state, mode of administration, mode of planning, types of programs offered, existence of complementary programs, program and agency history, reputation as to quality and performance, community and organizational structure, and community wealth. Needless to say, the dimensions used should be generally recognized as significant.

Another approach is to select sites that knowledgeable individuals regard as typical in the way they have dealt with the program. This *typical-site strategy* helps ensure that the results cannot be dismissed as peculiar to poor programs. Finding extensive problems in a sample of the worst hospitals in the state, for example, does not lead to credible statements about the extent of similar problems in other hospitals. Suggestions based on a sample of average-quality hospitals are likely to be more credible.

These two approaches to selecting sites were combined in a legislative evaluation of compensatory education in Connecticut, an exploratory study:

In selecting [three] local school districts for study, we tried to achieve diversity along certain background variables. Districts were chosen, first, that represent different community types. . . . Second, the districts chosen represent a range of populations. . . .

Finally, to protect against choosing a particularly unusual town, we asked state . . . officials about our choices, and were assured that no particular reasons existed for disqualifying the districts chosen.[6]

Of course, these protective measures do not allow you to generalize the conclusions across all sites, but a small, carefully drawn sample may provide some tentative, helpful insights into program characteristics. Or, as the Connecticut compensatory education evaluation put it:

. . . three school districts out of 165 does not a random sample make. As a result, it is impossible to make scientific generalizations or develop firm conclusions about state patterns. But by selecting towns meeting the diverse criteria set out above, the potential for discerning problems and successes that might exist in other towns is enhanced. . . .

Further investigation is required, or, perhaps more appropriately, legislative and administrative changes can be made to deal with the identified problems and to prevent them from occurring elsewhere.[7]

Hypothesis-Guided Evaluations

Diverse and typical sites can lead to suggestive findings. But when examining the plausibility of a narrow hypothesis about the characteristics of a program you might employ a less widely used approach—*crucial site* selection. Several crucial sites, carefully chosen and replicating one another, certainly won't demonstrate a hypothesis' generalizability to the satisfaction of statisticians. The inferences drawn, however, can be more credible than those from a few sites chosen without regard to their crucial characteristics. How much more credible, though, is debatable and an issue upon which reasonable people can differ.[8]

Suppose you wanted to demonstrate the plausibility of the hypothesis (which you think is true) that union domination is widespread in the day-to-day administration of schools. Suppose further that you can collect data in only two school districts—they will be the crucial sites. The problem is to pick sites that will be highly informative.

One possible choice would be school districts with unusually strong union contracts. But this choice would limit credible inferences—union domination found here would not inform conclusions about the level of union domination in the majority of school districts with weaker contracts. A second possibility would be to pick *typical* school districts, the approach often used in exploratory studies. If union domination of day-to-day management was found here, it certainly would lend more weight to the proposition about widespread union domination. But these results would not support conclusions about union domination in school districts with weak contracts. A third possibility, and sometimes the best one, is to pick *atypical* sites, school districts with unusually weak union contracts. If union domination of administration was found even in these unlikely settings, it would suggest that it existed in districts with stronger contracts and thus was widespread. This is a crucial site, an atypical site that contradicts prevailing expectations, if any site is likely to do so.

Another example comes from political science. Michels, in testing his hypothesis that oligarchy was universal in organizations, selected organizations dedicated to democratic principles and following democratic procedures. Because oligarchy prevailed even in these organizations, counter to prevailing expectations, Michels could argue persuasively that his proposition described widespread organizational behavior.

In both examples, the hypotheses being examined were assumed to be true. In such cases, a crucial site is one that is generally expected to refute the hypothesis. In other cases, however, if the analysts assume that a hypothesis is false, a crucial site is one that is generally expected to confirm the hypothesis. For example, if you are trying to disconfirm the widely held view that school districts are spending the state's special education funds on properly-selected children, crucial sites would be those expected to confirm the hypothesis, such as highly regarded districts reputed to follow state guidelines. Evidence that the money is being spent improperly in these districts would suggest that it is being spent improperly in less-highly regarded districts.

Practically speaking, how do you choose crucial sites? The process entails differentiating among various sites along dimensions relevant to the hypothesis. For example, the relevant dimensions in the Michels example were the democratic characteristics of organizations—things that could be specified and observed. Program dimensions that might be relevant and measurable include such things as agency size, salary level, organizational performance, expenditures per child, population characteristics, and efficiency ratings.

In many cases, however, identifying relevant dimensions and differentiating among them can be a problem. Suppose you are trying to locate crucial sites in which to examine a state program designed to computerize emergency room services in hospitals. Because the program calls for change, one relevant dimension might be the level of hospital innovation. But no scale exists to measure different levels of innovation, and it is not clear what organizational characteristic could act as a proxy. Staff-patient ratio? Number of young doctors? Per-day patient cost? Moreover, objective data on agency efficiency, performance, and quality might not exist.

Unfortunately for analysts, such problems are common in selecting crucial sites. A solution is to rely on *reputational data*, that is, the characteristics, behavior or performances of agencies as perceived by informed, respected sources. In the emergency room example, for instance, you could gather knowledgeable observers' opinions on the level of innovation of various hospitals. Other reputational data might focus on overall performance, efficiency, quality, responsiveness to clients, openness, stability or cooperation in carrying out state mandates.

The people whose opinions you seek for reputational data will depend on the subject of your study. In the emergency room example, they might be members of the state hospital commission or knowledgeable physicians. In other cases, they might be legislators, program administrators, recognized experts, or other informed observers. In asking for their opinions, you should try to identify several sites most expected to confirm or refute a hypothesis: reputational data are too imprecise to try to identify the single most likely site.

Selecting particular dimensions and choosing the individuals to rank the agencies are, of course, matters of judgment. These judgments can be flawed, leading to inaccurate conclusions. Even if appropriate dimensions are chosen, the imprecision of reputational data can create problems. It is possible, for example, to select a crucial site that, because of unusual or unknown factors, is an anomaly. In program evaluation, you need to be somewhat tentative in your conclusions. And it's wise to replicate your findings in as many crucial sites as possible.

Moreover, in the examples given earlier, the sites were truly crucial because the results turned out to be consistent with the working assumptions of the analysts, not with prevailing expectations. Alas, things do not always turn out that way, and when they don't, crucial sites can lead nowhere. Suppose Michels had not found oligarchy in his democractic organizations or that the special education funds were being properly spent in highly regarded districts. The results would not have led to a novel theory (Michels) or seriously questioned an accepted view (special education) because these hypothetical results would have matched prevailing expectations. What's more, such results would not add much to the validity of existing views. The fact that an extreme example (an expensive school that is well run) conforms to prevailing expectations is not nearly as informative as a less-extreme example (an average school that is well run).

So how do you avoid choosing sites that all turn out "the wrong way," giving you relatively useless results? You don't rely solely on the crucial site approach unless you are fairly confident of your assumption (expectation) that the results run counter to prevailing expectations. You won't know for sure until the results are in, so you're making a risky choice. If you are quite uncertain about the possible results, it might be best to back off entirely from atypical crucial sites and pick more typical ones. This limits your ability to generalize, but also makes it difficult to dismiss the results as extreme cases.

Practical Considerations

Whichever type of evaluation you're doing, a number of practical factors must be taken into account in selecting sites. Usually, the following questions should receive affirmative answers if a potential site is to be chosen for study. Are key on-site officials familiar with the operation and history of the program? Does the evaluation team have contacts at the site to help facilitate entry? Can the officials be convinced to cooperate? Has the site received sufficient funds from the program to have had ample experience in administration? Are the logistics of getting to the site and collecting data manageable? Taken as a whole, do the sites have believability (that is, do they look like a "good" sample to key political and program leaders)?[9]

There is one final practical consideration in selecting a sample—political horse sense. A true story of how *not* to proceed helps make the point. A legislative analyst set out to evaluate a state program that aided schools. Imbued with the canons of science and needing a sample, he turned to a table of random numbers to choose the schools for investigation. As it happened, one of the schools chosen was in the district of the subcommittee chairman who was the driving force behind the program evaluation. Not only that, the legislator was a school employee and partly responsible for the program under scrutiny. In effect, the legislator's activities became the subject of the evaluation. There was no need for this. A different school in the same category (size) could have been chosen just as easily without compromising the evaluation's integrity, and thus avoided a potentially embarrassing situation for the legislator. While such considerations should not dictate the inquiry, there is no need to unnecessarily aggravate the very individuals whom you want to use the results.

A Step-by-Step Illustration

It might be useful to conclude by going through the exercise of selecting sites for a hypothetical evaluation that combines many of the concerns discussed above. Suppose the legislature wants to explore the implementation of a relatively new education program for handicapped children. Suppose also that several key legislators would like to say something fairly definitive about their belief (hypothesis) that severely handicapped children are being shortchanged across the state; this perceived problem helped precipitate the evaluation. Suppose further that resources allow only three school districts to be visited and examined in depth. How do you choose the sites?

Because the evaluation is partly exploratory, you probably would want to adopt the diversity strategy. Your goal is to choose three districts that differ along several dimensions so the conclusions won't be limited to districts of the same character with the same problems. You might choose a suburban district, an urban district, and a rural one. In addition, the districts might differ in region, expenditure per child, and in the number of handicapped children served.

Because the evaluation is also examining the plausibility of a hypothesis—severely handicapped children are being shortchanged—you might try to identify crucial sites. If your working assumption is that the hypothesis is true, you will look for sites that are generally expected to refute the hypothesis—school districts that are reputed (say, by the state association for the handicapped) to have excellent programs for all types of handicapped children. But let's say, as is often the case, that you are not sure about the hypothesis—you think it might be invalid. If so, you might back off from the crucial sites, or you might hedge your bets by including a typical site, rather than having all the sites being somewhat extreme examples.

You generate several overlapping lists of potential sites, those that differ along several dimensions and those that are crucial-site possibilities. Combine the lists so the sample includes sites that are diverse, typical, and crucial. Then eliminate sites that don't pass the practical tests discussed earlier. The outcome of this juggling act should be a set of sites balanced as much as possible across the various criteria.

The final sites might include a large, urban district in the center of the state with many handicapped children and high expenditures, but with a reputation for having only an average program; a small rural district in the mountainous area of the state with low expenditures per child and few handicapped children, but a reputation for running an exemplary program; and a medium-sized, industrial, suburban district with high expenditures and a medium-sized, reputedly-strong program for the handicapped. Besides providing diversity, this sample has two sites (suburban and rural) generally expected to refute the hypothesis that the severely handicapped are being shortchanged, and one site (urban) generally thought to be typical.

Now let's consider some possible results from investigating these sites and try to interpret their meaning. Suppose you discover similar patterns of implementation in all three sites—difficulty in interpreting the law, problems created by late funding by the legislature, and trouble in following mandated procedures. Although the findings at three sites cannot be generalized to all settings, the diversity of sites allows you to suggest that these patterns might exist in other districts.

Suppose also that all three districts are doing an excellent job serving the severely handicapped. The fact that the suburban and rural districts are succeeding is not contrary to prevailing expectations. However, the fact that the urban district is doing an excellent job tends to undermine the original hypothesis that problems are widespread. Alternatively, suppose that all three districts are doing a poor job of serving the severely handicapped. This finding in the urban district is informative, but the fact that it is true in the highly-regarded suburban and rural districts lends a lot more credibility to the original hypothesis.

In short, by attending to crucial and typical sites, and to diversity, you can carefully select a small sample of sites that lead to tentative yet credible suggestions about statewide program implementation.

III. Getting In

Once sites have been selected, the next step is to get in, and to do so in a way that allows you to stay in. Accomplishing this can sometimes be tricky. It requires an understanding of the peculiar relationship between program evaluators and the host agencies being evaluated. And it requires strategies and tactics for sizing up the situation, making formal contact, and negotiating the terms of entry.

These issues are discussed below. Before turning to them, it should be noted that any single evaluation usually involves a series of negotiated entries for which you use varied strategies and tactics. You often need to establish relationships at different levels of hierarchical organizations. If there are different factions or power blocs within an agency, entry should be independentiy established with the staff in each of them. And analysts typically enter a number of organizations.[10] While learning strategies, remember that getting in sometimes is not a problem, but you can make it one. For example, some situations require no formal entry procedures—you just go ask people some questions. In such cases, a letter to an agency head requesting permission might create more problems. Indeed, in my judgment, getting into an organization and getting people to talk is easier than researchers commonly think. The idea is to think strategically, but not to overstrategize. On this issue as with many others in this book, there are no hard-and-fast rules. Good decisions on strategy reflect common sense and judgment, a sensitivity to the perspective of those being evaluated, and good intuition.

Evaluation Relationship

Imagine yourself as an official of the host organization. You are being asked (told) to share basic information about the inner workings of your program, ulcers and all. You are being asked not by academicians who will publish their findings in arcane journals, but by analysts who work for a body that controls the purse strings and seems preoccupied with efficiency and effectiveness. The analysts are evaluators; they are a threat; they are the enemy. Clearly, this basic character of the evaluation relationship can have a dramatic impact on entry and on the candor of agency officials.

While this portrait is generally accurate, it should also be noted that officials often cooperate because they are willing or want to, not just because they must. Some cooperate out of a sense of obligation; the public has a right to know how its money is being spent. Others cooperate because it provides them the opportunity to teach the evaluation's sponsors about program workings, because they believe the results will be informative. Still others might cooperate out of self-interest; certain information might help in internal power plays or be used to publicize their good work.

Finally, some organizational staffs cooperate simply because of the low salience of the information requested. For example, if you were examining a program operated by the state education department and needed statistics from the welfare department, this welfare data might be made available without difficulty.

A safe working assumption is that different people will cooperate for a variety of complex reasons that frequently are not obvious. It would be a mistake to equate cordiality with candor or permission to enter with access to what's really happening. The more you can look at the evaluation relationship from the agency officials' perspective, the more your entry strategies and tactics will be on target.

Sizing Up the Site

Preliminary scouting assures that when formal contact is made, it is done in the right way with the appropriate people.

The best source of information is a known contact within the organization. Ideally, this person would be a friend or trusted acquaintance who knows his way around the organization; knowledge is a lot more important than status. This contact might provide straightforward information about what procedures to follow. In some organizations, it is appropriate to go directly to the subunit administrator in charge of the program. In others, standard procedures govern research relationships; before getting in, you may have to be cleared by the front office. The contact might also provide confidential predictions about how different program people will react to the evaluation and make recommendations about how to proceed. Certain individuals in any organization are more disposed to evaluations than others; they may have less to hide, something to show off, or a highly developed sense of obligation. Other things being equal, it makes sense to avoid threatened parties and negotiate entry through individuals sympathetic to the evaluation.

In addition, the contact might provide political advice. For example, you might be legally entitled to enter a respected hospital to examine program administration. However, it might make political sense to first approach hospital officials as if permission to enter were required. Agency contacts might also act as internal sponsors for the evaluation. A contact who vouches for your integrity and is trusted by fellow employees can provide a great service by reducing anxieties.

If an internal contact is not available, you can find someone outside who is knowledgeable about the organization and ask for advice on how to proceed. For example, if the evaluation involves studying several mental institutions, you might contact a former public health official who has a statewide perspective.

Also helpful in sizing up the situation will be the documents you are reading about the organization. The methodology section of an earlier report on the agency might describe how others gained entry. The recent release of a highly critical report on an organization should put you on the alert for entry problems ahead—once burned, always wary, and the agency may now stiffly resist any analysts. Information about a criticized agency might even lead to the selection of another site.

Making Formal Contact

Once sites have been chosen and sized up, the appropriate analyst to make formal contact must be picked. Normally the team leader should initiate contact, especially in situations where the authority of his position may influence the success of the contact. For example, a school superintendent might view a visit by a research assistant as an insult. Alternatively, a contact might be chosen on the basis of an ability to make a strong first impression. Successful entry depends not only upon authority, but on the establishment of rapport. An analyst who easily displays a friendly manner, a willingness to listen, and a genuine interest in the truth can help overcome agency fears about being evaluated. If neither of these approaches makes sense, the sponsor of the evaluation can make the contact, thus directly asserting the authority of the undertaking.

The next step is to actually make formal contact with the appropriate agency officials. You should know from the scouting whether an approach by telephone, in person, or by letter is likely to be the most effective. For example, a personal visit from a team member might be necessary to signal the seriousness of the evaluation; it is less casual than a telephone call. It also establishes face-to-face contact and provides an opportunity to bargain about the details of the entry. Logistics can affect your decision. An agency across the street from the legislature might expect a visit, for example, while an agency 200 miles across the state might not.

Regardless of who makes the formal contact or how, the contact person needs to identify who he represents—the sponsor—and who will do the study—the analysts. The purpose of the evaluation should be explained in simple language, in a nonthreatening way. One good approach is to say that the evaluation is intended to understand the program with the hope of improving it. This quick introduction and explanation may be all that is needed.

Negotiating Entry

Sometimes, however, the host organization raises questions about the terms of entry; the first formal contact is just the first inning in a bargaining game. Be prepared to explain why the evaluation is being carried out, how the data will be used, how individuals will be protected, what the risks are, and how the host organization was chosen. Indeed, many analysts believe they are always obligated to provide this type of basic information.* In

*In Chapter 7, I discuss the analyst's responsibilities for treating agencies and individuals fairly.

trying to persuade the host organization to permit entry, you might also point to completed evaluations that demonstrate the protection of the individuals and agencies involved, or you might identify individuals within the agency who are familiar with your work and integrity. Name-dropping may be obnoxious in social settings, but it is a valued tactic in field research. Although all this information should be presented simply and honestly, you should not feel obliged to volunteer details about current hypotheses, hunches, or possible conclusions.

You can further facilitate entry by appealing to the host agency's motivation to cooperate, or by promising to collect and share information the agency needs. In addition, a variety of assurances can be offered that might reduce resistance without unduly interfering with the evaluation. One promise is to share the penultimate draft with agency officials, so they can correct mistakes and dispute interpretations prior to publication. A second is to promise agency officials the opportunity to write a formal rebuttal that will be attached to the published evaluation. A third promise is to sit down and go over the findings before the evaluation is released. In some states, these three assurances are offered as part of standard procedures, not as concessions in bargaining.

Finally, you might consider making detailed promises about confidentiality. For example, rather than identifying sites, fictitious names will be used; sources will not be revealed or quoted by name; confidential documents will not be pursued; off-the-record statements will not be quoted. Also, you can promise to respect the demands on the time of busy officials and to minimize disruption. Simply acknowledging these problems is a step toward establishing good relations.

However, be careful with your assurances, and do not promise what cannot be delivered. Do you know that you will have time to share data with the host agency? Can top officials be promised confidentiality in an investigation of *their* program? Can quotes be used without indirectly revealing the source? Will a fictitious name sufficiently conceal the identity of a town or an agency? Can key agencies or towns be promised that a fictitious name will be used? Can the agency realistically expect to reap the benefits promised from the evaluation results?

Besides these practical considerations, there are legal ones. Confidential material collected during an evaluation could be subpoenaed, although it seems highly unlikely in most evaluations. Refusal to cooperate could conceivably lead to imprisonment. This has happened to newspaper reporters who refused to reveal their sources. What's more, the federal Freedom of Information Act could apply to your evaluation if it was federally funded; confidential documents in the hands of a federal agency have been made public over the objection of researchers.[11] But the Act apparently does not extend to confidential documents that are not in the possession of a federal agency. Before offering assurances of confidentiality, consider the possible interest of the courts in your data, develop procedures to protect confidential material, and check the evolving law in this area.[12]

At bottom, the negotiated settlement should provide the information and assurances that are both necessary for entry and ethically required to protect agency officials against unnecessary risks. Avoid commitments that would seriously constrain the search for truth or would violate promises of confidentiality. Promises made should be honored, although the agreement should be flexible enough to permit renegotiation after the evaluation is under way.[13]

3

Coping with Bias
and Error

T HE NEXT STEP in an evaluation involves going into the field and actually collecting data that are accurate, relevant, reasonably complete and, if the study is repeated by other investigators, consistent with their findings.[1] Doing this requires not only the skilled application of data-collecting techniques, but also an understanding of an impressive list of things that can contaminate the results. So, before turning to data-collecting techniques in the next two chapters, I explore here, first, some major *sources* of bias and error and then, some general *safeguards* for dealing with them. Although fieldwork methods are often criticized for being especially susceptible to bias and error, systematic procedures do exist for coping with these potential problems.[2]

I. SOURCES OF BIAS AND ERROR

An analyst who doesn't identify sources of bias and error in evaluating a program is like a surgeon who ignores germs and infection while performing an operation. Both will encounter complications that produce harmful results. In program evaluation, the possible complications can originate with the analyst himself, with the subjects (those being interviewed or observed), and the situation in which the data are (or are not) being collected. Let's take a look at major problems in each of these three categories.

The Analyst

Researchers in many fields can draw upon predesigned instruments for collecting data. These might be achievement tests to measure reading ability, scales to measure the weight of objects, or rulers to measure length. But such standardized devices are not available for the type of program evaluation emphasized in this book. There are few rulers to measure the decision-making process, or scales to weigh political forces. In this case, the analyst is the instrument—he watches, hears, reads, and records without benefit of a predefined, prevalidated device.

Consequently, the analyst and the background he applies to his work, knowingly or not, can profoundly influence the choice of information collected, whether it is free from error, and how it is interpreted. Seven important sources of bias and error are highlighted here.

Methods used   A given analyst generally favors a given method for collecting data. My own bias toward intensive interviewing is reflected in this book. But the exclusive use of any one method can lead to selective, distorted results. Intensive interviewing sacrifices breadth of coverage for depth and can lead to faulty generalizations. Structured questionnaires sacrifice depth for breadth and can produce inaccurate portraits of the inner workings of a program. Data based on observation is skewed toward the present because one obviously cannot directly observe the past. Documents published by an agency might provide facts, propaganda, or a combination of the two.

Data collection methods should be matched to the question, not the reverse. The problem is that some analysts know but one method, resulting in what Abraham Kaplan calls the law of the instrument: Give a would-be carpenter only a hammer and he will find things to pound—including an unassuming screw.[3] Clearly, you should have a kit of research tools, and you should know their functions, strengths and weaknesses, and know the questions they can address.

Conceptual framework   As noted in Chapter 1, different people hold different assumptions about how the government works and what is important. For example, some analysts view interpersonal relationships as central while others focus on rational procedures for making decisions. These assumptions (or conceptual frameworks) affect both what is seen and reported, and how data are interpreted. This means that two analysts with two different conceptual frameworks could write different stories about the same program. The different stories would not be wrong, rather, each would be biased by the use of a different conceptual lens.

Predispositions   Apart from his conceptual framework, the analyst's opinions, attitudes, beliefs, values, motivations, expectations, and prejudices can lead to serious distortions and omissions. For example, if you believe your boss is opposed to the program, you might see and hear primarily the negative evidence you think he wants, filtering out the positive. If you expect a particular site to be crucial, you might ignore data calling this assumption into question. If the subject talks your language—he appears articulate, analytic, reflective—you might be too ready to accept his views. If you want to protect a friend, you might overstate the program's value. These distortions might be either unconscious or deliberate.

Feelings   Evaluations don't involve just cognitive processes, although methodology sections of reports usually make it sound that way. Analysts' feelings can also influence observations substantially. As a novice, you might fear making a fool of yourself on your first day of interviewing. You might feel guilty evaluating a program rather than serving its needy clients. You might be anxious about being an unwanted outsider. You might be nervous about whether you'll ever find anything and ever finish. You might feel exhausted from overwork. One analyst's field notes record his feelings:

> ...even though I probably appear cucumber-cool to everyone down there, I am, for the most part, scared to death of some of those people, and in many cases I don't know any good reason for this. Every morning around seven forty-five, as I'm driving to the office, I begin to get this pain in the left side of my back, and the damn thing stays there usually until around eleven.... But I guess that the biggest thing that keeps gnawing at me is Bonnie's reaction to my presence in the office. Man, if I would've had any idea at all before I began this damn project that a field researcher could possibly cause someone so much grief, you can bet that I wouldn't be here.[4]

In addition, you might develop strong feelings about the individuals involved in the project. You might resent that they have more interesting jobs, dislike the way they behave, detest their attitude toward program clients, admire them for their courage, or respect them for their dedication. For example, you might over-identify with the program administrators—a condition described as "going native" by anthropologists—and start to act as a defense attorney for them. The result could be a one-sided story.

Feelings can bias perceptions in ways that are not entirely understood. Recognizing their existence rather than denying them is an essential first step toward figuring out their impact.

Ignorance Problems can arise when the analyst is unfamiliar with the norms, customs, and traditions that affect the program being evaluated. When such ignorance is combined with an unexamined value orientation, embarrassing mistakes can easily result. For instance, in conducting an evaluation on an island in Micronesia, I was startled to discover that children at a boarding school were sleeping on wooden platforms rather than mattresses. Later I learned that this practice reflected local mores. Had I interpreted this in light of Western values, as I almost did, I would have been guilty of mistaking a custom for a problem.

Environmental factors   Other influences that help shape the ways in which a program is perceived and reported include the norms, traditions, and values of the historical time, the cultural milieu, the political environment, and the organization in which the analyst works. A program's being labeled a failure or a success is partly a function of the prevailing mood, and the general level of societal optimism. For example, the "failure" of the War on Poverty might reflect dashed expectations as much as the actual results.

Incompetence   Of course the untrained, inexperienced analyst can easily bungle the asking of questions, the interpretation of answers, the observation of events, the follow-up on crucial points, the recording of data, the presentation of a useful report. The result can be an analyst confident about "the facts" but dead wrong about what actually happened.

In sum, the field evaluator is a rather complicated instrument for filtering program information. Either unconsciously or deliberately, he can produce an evaluation that is inaccurate, unreliable, misleading, or slanted. The conscientious analyst would do well to assess how these sources of bias and error can affect his own work, and employ the safeguards discussed later.

The Subject

Bias and error can also originate with those who provide the information—those interviewed or observed, and those who write the documents that provide written evidence for the evaluation. As with analysts, the subjects' conceptual frameworks, predispositions, feelings, ignorance, environment, and competence can influence how they perceive and report on a program. With that understood, this section examines potential problems in a different light. This concerns subjects who are *unable* to provide accurate information and subjects who are *unwilling* to cooperate. Either can cause major problems. A combination of the two can play havoc with the pursuit of an accurate portrayal of a program.

Ability   A subject may participate willingly in an interview but not be able to give accurate information, either because he can't answer the questions completely, or because he unknowingly provides inaccurate data.

As an example of someone who is unable to give complete answers, consider an administrator who has suppressed a horrendous struggle with parents in implementing a new program for their children. Now, the details of the experience escape him.

Another subject's responses might be incomplete because he is unable to report on repetitious routine behavior that he is scarcely conscious of. Or, he may neglect to point out important standards and procedures that he takes for granted in his work.

The subject may be unable to respond because he has simply forgotten. In the human memory, many events, like leaky boats, gradually sink out of sight. As a general rule, the longer the time between an event and a request for its recall, the more that will be forgotten. An event that seemed inconsequential will usually be forgotten more quickly than one that seemed important.

The inability of a subject to respond for these reasons can lead to an incomplete report. But the analyst usually will be aware that the requested information has not been provided, and can try to collect it in other ways. A much more serious problem arises when the subject doesn't know the answers, and, in the mistaken belief that he does, unintentionally gives erroneous information.

To avoid this, it might seem a good strategy to rely on subjects with direct, firsthand evidence. After all, we've learned from Perry Mason that the best person to put on the stand is an eyewitness. But research has demonstrated that even eyewitnesses can be unreliable. Indeed, authorities estimate that when the average person reports on conversations and events from memory, about ten to twenty-five percent of his statements will be unintentionally inaccurate.[5] This is also true in program evaluation. Many subjects, while presenting their direct observations with certainty and honesty, are actually quite off the mark.

One reason for this might be that the subject is simply a poor observer. Or, even if he is a good eyewitness, he might jump to erroneous conclusions. His inferences might simply be illogical. Or they might be triggered by strongly-held views, and thus reflect his predispositions more than the actual occurrence.

Another reason might be self-deception. It is common, for example, for top administrators to deceive themselves, believing they know what is going on in their organizations. When they really don't know but think they do, the information they give can obviously add error to the findings.

Still another reason is that people often misremember events involving habitual behavior. This is well illustrated in the true story of a man named Twitchell who was convicted of murder based on false testimony, honestly given, involving a habit. After killing his wife, Twitchell unlocked the front gate to his house to make it appear as if an intruder had committed the crime. Twitchell's servant, who was in the habit of unlatching the gate each morning, swore in court that she had unlatched the gate as she ran for the police; her daily habit was sincerely, but erroneously incorporated into her testimony.*

Finally, we know that people just forget that they have forgotten—but a fertile imagination, suggestion, or desire can make their "memories" seem real. Dull tales become interesting. Gaps in a story are filled in with what might have happened. Hearsay is remembered as direct experience. Confusing and uncertain plans are recalled as logical, coherent, rational acts. This is why research on problems of recall refers to the "treachery of

---

*Twitchell was sent to prison. He later admitted his guilt and, while awaiting execution, committed suicide by eating the poison-soaked pages of a Bible brought to him by a friend.[6]

recollection," "selective recall," and the "reconstruction of biography."

Subject cooperation   Sometimes subjects who are able to provide accurate information about the issue being investigated are simply unwilling to cooperate. First, the subject might resist cooperating because honest answers would violate norms and accepted practices. For example, discussing interpersonal problems is considered inappropriate in many organizations even though these problems may have been instrumental in a program's failure. It might seem improper to speak critically about a program; politeness might stifle candid appraisals. It might be thought wrong to report on political maneuvering within an organization even though it might be rampant. Or the subject might avoid disagreeing with the analyst; courtesy to outsiders could soften the answers.

Second, the subject might be unwilling to respond honestly or behave normally because he has a different agenda than you. For example, a high-ranking official or program officer would typically act as an advocate, accentuating the positive. Or the subject might want to use the interview to pursue some personal goals unrelated to the evaluation (for example, to get information about jobs, or to gain your favor).

Third, the subject might be unwilling because he feels personally threatened. He might be nervous, tense, or frightened because he doesn't know what's expected. He might be fearful about having to discuss an upsetting experience. He might foresee that honest answers would be embarrassing because they would reveal his ignorance, mistakes, or failings. Subjects will avoid these threats to their image and self-esteem.

Finally, the subject might be unwilling to cooperate because he fears the consequences. For example, the release of sensitive program data could adversely affect a program's future, its funding, and the people who run it. The subject might not trust you and fear that the public report will misquote him, embarrass him, or misinterpret what he said. An employee might fear for his job if he speaks openly in front of his boss or if it is learned that he talked candidly with you. Or the subject might fear legal consequences if he is being questioned about the possible misuse of public money.

Unwilling to cooperate for any of these reasons, the subject might straightforwardly refuse to participate. Less directly, he may be "too busy" to be of much help, arriving late, leaving early, or encouraging interruptions.

Typically, the subject tries to hide his unwillingness. One way is to avoid disclosing the full truth by evading the interviewer's questions through the clever use of silence, partial answers, superficialities, irrelevancies, or the literal truth.[7] He acts as if he is presenting the whole truth and nothing but the truth, while in fact he is intentionally deceiving the analyst. He may provide "iceberg" answers—most of the truth is below the surface. In such cases, it should be obvious that if a subject, particularly a program advocate, points to a problem, it usually means a big problem, and an admitted big problem often points to a real disaster.

A second means by which subjects try to hide their uncooperativeness is by presenting a front. For example, the rational master plans of an agency may conceal internal political bargaining. Everyone within the organization knows what is happening but the front of rational procedures is maintained for the outsider. This is common human behavior—analysts themselves are not disinclined to use fronts. Most program evaluation involves mistakes, false starts and logistical blunders; yet it is common to describe the process as if everything went smoothly according to plan.

A third hiding device is the baldfaced lie. But the subject who lies runs the risk of evidence turning up to disprove him. From my experience and observation, while subjects occasionally lie (depending on the issue, available alternatives, and the stakes involved), evasion is more common. It is a lot easier for a subject to recover from an evasive statement than from a discovered lie.

I do not mean to portray the subjects of program evaluation as unusually devious and conniving souls—most are trying to do their best by their own lights. But it is important for you to be aware of possible pitfalls and to be on guard.

The Situation

In a given situation, there are two primary sources of bias and error in addition to all those that can originate with the analyst and the subject individually.

Perhaps the most important source is the result of combining the two individuals—the subject's reaction to the presence of the analyst. The subject either acts in ways that are not normal or provides answers that do not reflect his true views. This serious, often-found problem is normally referred to as reactivity or the *Hawthorne effect*.[8] The latter name comes from a famous experiment in the 1930s that examined the factors affecting worker productivity in the Hawthorne plant. The experimenters found that regardless of the level of lighting, monetary incentives, or pattern of management, the workers were more productive than usual. They were reacting to the presence of the experimenters, not the variation in working conditions.

In program evaluation, the analyst brings to the research not only a set of questions (or the desire to observe), but also a particular identity—age, race, sex, socioeconomic status, ethnic group, personality, manner, and ideas. What's more, the analyst is not just another person; he is an outsider, an evaluator, a potential threat. These things make the subject self-conscious about his own behavior, and affect what the subject perceives, what role he takes, and how he responds to the analyst. What group of students does not perform for the outside observer? In a different type of situation, the presence of a black analyst asking a lot of questions in a white community, or a white in a black community, could affect the willingness of those being interviewed to cooperate or to answer questions fully and honestly. An analyst's overbearing personality, haughty manner or unusual dress, rather than the question, might capture the subject's attention and thought. Or the subject might end up reacting to the analyst's reactions, rather than responding to the questions.

This potential problem is not a one-way street. An analyst also reacts to more than the subject's answers or behavior. His impressions and expectations of the subject all influence the kinds and number of questions asked. Stated differently, a change of analysts could produce strikingly different results.

Another problem is omission. Because fieldwork is designed to explore issues in depth, it naturally has to be selective and the number of sites visited is usually quite small. Within these sites only a small number of events are observed, only a few people are interviewed, and only some documents are read. Furthermore, despite careful planning, what one sees and hears is shaped in part by the particular day, season of the year, or period in the program's history. What this means, of course, is that a lot is never seen, heard, or read. It also means that what is observed may not be representative behavior. These omitted data, if gathered, might create a different picture of the program.

In conclusion, this list of potential sources of bias and error associated with the research situation, the analyst, and the subject should give pause to the program evaluator who might be confident about his findings and interpretations. What's more, this list is not exhaustive. No doubt there are other problems associated with the unconscious that we do not even know about, much less how to articulate.

II. SAFEGUARDS AGAINST BIAS AND ERROR

It is not enough to be aware of the various possible sources of bias and error and to recognize the uncertainties in collecting valid information. You need to identify specific sources, monitor and evaluate their effects, and take steps to deal with them. Sometimes the proper course is to acknowledge your bias because it is part of the process. For example, the analyst's conceptual framework biases the results; the underlying assumptions should be articulated. Other times, you will try to reduce or eliminate bias and error by employing safeguards. Some of these safeguards—an evaluative frame of mind, data quality controls, and feedback on your work—are discussed below. Others, tied to specific data collection methods, are discussed in Chapters 4 and 5.

An Evaluative Frame of Mind

Dealing with bias and error requires a particular frame of mind, a probing stance by the analyst toward both himself and his data. It calls for self-awareness, self-examination, and self-discipline that go beyond what is required in ordinary life. You must be willing to examine your predispositions, feelings, values, skills, shortcomings, and assumptions. This introspection takes the form of questioning: What do I really think of the program? Am I being fair? Do I understand the agency perspective, even if I don't agree with it? Am I inclined to find the program a failure? Why? To help my career? Why am I having trouble getting Al Brown to talk? Is it me? My presence? What data am I including or excluding from the report? Why? Why those assumptions, not others? Have I been consistent as an observer over time?

Beyond introspective questioning, you must be willing to suspend judgment, to hold in check your opinions, values, attitudes, and conclusions in an effort to impartially collect and analyze program data. This means that you try to get outside yourself, detached from the program and what you bring to it, and consciously search for evidence designed to counteract your feelings and disconfirm your predispositions and hypotheses.

Finally, you must adopt a hard-nosed attitude about the validity of the data, one that is at once benign and skeptical. It is benign in that the evaluation's purpose is not to embarrass bureaucrats or to harrass the executive branch, but to come as close as possible to the truth. It is skeptical because only that attitude will ensure the continual questioning of the data required to arrive at an accurate report. A skeptical analyst challenges what he sees, hears, and reads.

He questions assumptions, seeks direct and confirming evidence, searches for holes in the data, makes the familiar strange, and tries to turn accepted arguments on their head. To quote British historian Herbert Butterfield, you "must be as jealous and importunate as the cad of a detective who has to find the murderer amongst a party of his friends."[9]

Data Quality Control

A second set of safeguards involves specific procedures for gathering appropriate information and assessing its quality while it is being collected. The skilled analyst will carefully assess each piece of data, cross-check and corroborate the data with different sources, and "triangulate" by using multiple methods to further corroborate important points.

You must apply a variety of tests to each piece of information collected, to gauge the level of confidence that can be placed in each account or observation.[10] The first test focuses on plausibility. Does the story or observation make sense? Is it reasonable? Do the pieces fit together? While truth is sometimes stranger than fiction, it is also a fact that analysts often accept false stories or contrived behavior because they fail to focus on plausibility.

A second test focuses on consistency. Does the account contradict itself? Is the account or behavior consistent with what the analyst already knows? The assumption is that internal contradiction might be a sign of evasion or lying.

A third test focuses on the differential level of certainty of an account. One can assume that a subject knows different things with different levels of confidence and that these differences should be reflected in his story. Does the subject assert things with varying levels of confidence? Does the subject acknowledge what he knows and what he does not?

A fourth test focuses on the level of detail in the account. The assumption is that if the subject says he knows something thoroughly, he should be able to describe it in minute detail. Is the story rich with details? Is it precise? Can the subject recall the specific circumstances? In interviewing, depth of information can be tested by pressing the subject for more details even if they are inconsequential.

A fifth test focuses on the account's interconnectedness. The assumption is that descriptions of things that are truly known connect facts, actors, meanings, and contexts. Are key factors woven together? Are relationships discussed? Does the story hold together?

A sixth test focuses on whether the data reflect direct experience. Is the subject's story an eyewitness account or hearsay? Was he in a position to get a full picture of what happened? Direct evidence is usually more reliable than second or thirdhand accounts.

A final test focuses not on the account, but on the subject. Does he display the characteristics of a good observer—detached, not driven by predispositions, self-critical, not self-serving? Does the subject comprehend questions? Does he appear willing to participate? Does he seem to be reacting naturally, rather than to the presence of the analyst? From past experience, is the subject known as a reliable observer?

If all these questions can be answered "yes," it is likely that the individual account or observed behavior will have the ring of truth and you can feel confident about your data. More likely, though, some of the answers will be "yes," others "maybe," and still others "no." You will sense that things don't quite fit or you may have specific hunches about what is wrong. Regardless of the level of confidence, important facts and interpretations need to be verified, and conclusions need to be corroborated. Usually, this can be done by seeking disconfirming evidence from two or more independent sources. If the sources are truly independent, it is unlikely (although not impossible) that they would say the same thing unless their observations were accurate. (Similarly, observational data from a single site, for instance from a classroom, can be corroborated by observing the class at other times chosen at random.)

Even when good sources corroborate one another, the truth can still be distorted because a single method was used (for example during interviewing all the subjects were trying to please the interviewer). Further verification and corroboration can be obtained through an important method called triangulation.[11] It consists of getting a reading on a particular fact from different angles using different data-gathering techniques. For example, interviews might provide you with a mental picture of how the project works. You could triangulate this view by checking it out through direct observations and document analysis. If each of the methods points to the same conclusion, this suggests that the initial view is accurate. Triangulation is time-consuming, but quite important, particularly for corroborating crucial matters.

Feedback on Your Work

In addition to these procedures for assessing data, you must also seek feedback from various sources on the conduct of the evaluation and on the findings and conclusions as they approach final form. The purpose is to reduce your bias and sharpen your argument.

The fresh eye of a neutral colleague, not caught up in the evaluation, can identify problems with the data and interpretations that someone knee-deep in the analysis cannot see. An outsider can point to implausible data, holes in the argument, leaps of logic, and alternative interpretations. Often the most important points are buried in the report; a colleague can suggest ways that they can be highlighted. This critical role can also be played by a member of the evaluation team who might have concentrated on another part of the evaluation. If he comes at the data from a different perspective, all the better for the development of alternative ways of presenting the material.

Most important, a neutral colleague (or team member) can play a crucial role in helping the analyst reduce his personal biases. Discussions of predispositions and feelings can help identify their impact on the analyst's perceptions. An uninvolved peer, for example, can spot an analyst who is "going native" or who is reacting unfairly because he doesn't like the subjects. A colleague can suggest ways to compensate for these identified biases (for example, interview additional people or check out a rival interpretation). All this feedback can take the form of tough criticism that can wound the pride, but is essential to maintaining a balanced perspective.

Finally, bias and error can be reduced by sharing the penultimate draft with the key individuals whose program is the focus of the evaluation. The purpose is to allow them to respond to the "final facts" in the context of the evaluation document. Sharing the draft almost inevitably leads to claims of unfair treatment, if the report is at all critical. To buttress their charges, administrators will point to inaccuracies in the draft. The way to deal with this is to discuss the mistakes and different interpretations, changing the draft where the administrators' facts and arguments are persuasive. Also, it is often appropriate to provide the executive with space in the final report for a written rebuttal.

This draft-sharing takes time, but it is essential in clarifying issues and eliminating errors. It is usually the last procedure used for reducing your bias and corroborating the data.

4

Intensive Interviewing

IT'S NOW TIME to discuss the principles and procedures governing the collection of data by various techniques. In this chapter, I focus on intensive interviewing, the most time-consuming method used. In the next chapter, I discuss two additional data-gathering procedures: transient observation and document analysis. Used together, these three methods allow you to figure out systematically, if imperfectly, what's really going on in the program and why.

Interviewing can be loosely defined as a conversation with a purpose. In program evaluation you aim to elicit accurate, relevant, and reasonably complete information about a program. Some interviews are highly structured and standardized, with the questions worked out in advance and asked in a fixed order. This type of interviewing, associated with surveys, questionnaires and polls, does not concern us here. What we're interested in are free-flowing, open-ended interviews, probing for more and more detail. This type of interviewing has been labeled unstructured, semistructured, nonstandardized, in-depth, elite, exploratory, journalistic, intensive—these terms all reflect its character. None of these labels is totally satisfactory, but the label of *intensive* interviewing captures the thoroughness of the approach and the concerted effort required, not only to gather quality information, but also to collect lively quotations and interesting anecdotes, to capture the life, spirit and color of the government program in action. This chapter examines a number of techniques and safeguards to remember when collecting the desired information.

There is no one best way to conduct intensive interviews. That depends on the evaluation issues, the situation, the context in which the interview takes place, and the subjects as they react to it all. Even given the same set of circumstances, there is no one best way for different individuals to handle an interview. That depends on the personality, background, knowledge, and style of the analyst. Just as baseball players adopt distinctive swings that work for them, analysts need to devise procedures that match the characteristics they bring to interviewing.

Presented here is a contingency approach to interviewing; the choice of procedures depends on your assessment of various situational and personal factors. In some cases, you will have time to carefully assess the contingencies and rationally consider alternative approaches. More often, though, split-second decisions must be made, one right after another, during the interview itself. Good interviewing, then, requires an understanding of procedures, adaptability to contingencies, and, at bottom, quick guessing and good intuition.

Although these things cannot be reduced to formulas, it is possible to examine some issues that would-be interviewers need to think about, and to discuss some procedures that often work. Toward that end, this chapter addresses getting ready for the interviews, getting started and setting the tone, asking good questions, challenging the subject if need be, and finishing up. It is up to you to assess the situation, to analyze your strengths, and to experiment with procedures that seem to fit.[1]

I. GETTING READY

Is intensive interviewing the most appropriate method? Who should be interviewed, when, where, and by whom? How can appointments be arranged? What homework needs to be done? How will the data be recorded? This section elaborates on such strategic questions.

Why Intensive Interviewing?

The first step in getting ready is to pause for a moment and ask why interviewing has been chosen. Does it seem to be the most appropriate, efficient method for collecting the kinds of data required? Interviewing is labor-intensive, difficult for novices to do well, hard to synchronize among interviewers, and, given limited time, leaves lots of areas uncovered because it involves in-depth analysis rather than broad coverage. Interviewing can produce biased data because the subject may be responding to your presence rather than presenting an accurate account. Furthermore, it is an inefficient means for collecting basic statistics, or for gathering a broad range of opinion or attitudinal information. Thus, intensive interviewing is inappropriate as the major data-gathering technique in many situations.

But there are many situations in which intensive interviewing is the best method. One of these is when you are interested in examining issues of process—how decisions were made, or how the program has evolved. Another is when you intend to examine the reasons for complex events, the context in which a project was put into operation, or what the program means to key participants and influentials. Still others are when all the questions cannot be anticipated and when subjects may be unwilling or unable to cooperate. The strength of interviewing is its flexibility; you can adjust to evolving circumstances, add subjects as the study moves along, and keep probing until you get the facts. Intensive interviewing is an exploratory tool that can get at the nitty-gritty of program operations, revealing what actually happened, why, and with what impact. It is not the only tool, nor is it meant to be used for needless fishing expeditions. But intensive interviewing is ideally suited to gathering data about crucial steps in program implementation.

Picking the Subjects

If intensive interviewing is definitely your choice, the next step is to figure out whom to interview. Two types of individuals are sought. One type is what anthropologists call a key informant. Such individuals are quite familiar with the program and its environment; they know the key figures, the problems, the successes, the norms, and the traditions. They also are reliable observers who have the time and the inclination to meet with you. An informant can judge the reliability of potential interviewees, suggest people to talk with, make introductions, propose tactics for collecting information, and react to collected data and tentative interpretations. An ideal informant can help you as a tactician, a behind-the-scenes advisor, a sounding board, a confidant, and a tremendous source of information. If—and this is a big if—you can find informants whose information checks out, they can make the evaluation job much easier, and the results a lot more accurate.

The second type of subject is the regular interviewee, one of many individuals you will meet with at least once or twice. These relationships normally are more formal than with key informants and involve less time. Most of this chapter focuses on these relationships.

The selection of subjects depends in part on the evaluation questions. If the questions focus on program operation and impact, administrators and clients should be interviewed. If they concern the bureaucratic and political milieu, knowledgeable individuals in the legislature and the bureaucracy, as well as outside government, ought to be consulted. If the questions center on program evolution, seek out old-timers who have had firsthand experience with the program over the years. If the questions concern program success, talk to individuals with comparable experience (someone who has worked in several states, school districts, or hospitals). In choosing subjects to answer any of these questions, don't forget to interview former legislators or former program administrators. Those who have vacated positions of authority are frequently more willing to talk candidly (although they also can have jaundiced views).

You should, of course, seek a variety of perspectives on key issues, and you will discover a striking variety as you get deeper into the study. This "wagon train" strategy of surrounding issues with interviews is essential in capturing the truth.[2] Because there is something to the aphorism that "where one sits determines where one stands," organizational affiliation and position provide a rough preliminary guide to who stands where. For example, you would expect an agency official to be a program advocate, so part of what he says can probably be discounted. Alternative perspectives might be provided by an appropriations committee analyst, a local client, a newspaperman, a lobbyist, or an advocacy-group representative.

Differing views are also likely to come from lower-level personnel in the agency, who may well be among your best sources. High-level officials should be interviewed because of their wide perspective and firsthand knowledge of how top-level decisions are made. But such officials, experienced in public speaking and giving interviews, are often adept at responding to questions without answering them. In contrast, lower-level employees are more familiar with day-to-day operations, are often less guarded, and may find more time for interviewing and reinterviewing. It is usually among these ranks, rather than among program spokespeople, that you find key informants.

Ideally, interviewees are reliable sources of data, with firsthand knowledge of the topic and the willingness, if motivated and prodded, to talk freely and candidly. Some are central figures identified from the start. Others are identified as data are collected, new hypotheses are formed, hunches are developed, and names are suggested by both interviewees and informants. Picking a sample as the study rolls along is commonly and aptly referred to as "snowball sampling." Finally, other individuals become subjects serendipitously. When I arrived for one interview, for example, I was told that the official had been called away on an emergency. His workmate, whom I thought knew nothing about the program, volunteered to fill the void. Mainly out of politeness I agreed to meet with him, only to have the best interview of the project.

Besides picking subjects, you must also consider whether they should be interviewed individually, in pairs or in groups. In interviews involving more than one person at a time, different perspectives can be presented and debated, often yielding more information than a series of individual interviews. Also, you can gather a wider array of opinions in a shorter period of time. There are, however, many disadvantages. Some subjects become less candid in the presence of others, particularly their bosses; they avoid threatening, revealing, controversial material. Also, contradictory accounts can be adjusted on-the-spot to project a consistent view, and you may miss hearing the contradictions. Finally, it is quite difficult to record the session because more than one person is often talking at the same time. On balance, I prefer to interview individuals one at a time. Toward the end of a study, however, a group session to discuss tentative findings can be quite productive.

Picking the Interviewers

If your evaluation project is staffed by a team, it is worth giving some thought to who interviews whom, because subjects can respond as much to the characteristics of the interviewer as to the questions asked. Assure compatability between the interviewer and the subject as much as possible to minimize interaction effects that might distort the data. Moreover, some analysts are more adept at interviewing than others—they establish instant rapport, they have a knack for getting people to talk, and they evaluate answers quickly. If possible, these interviewers should concentrate on the more difficult subjects.

Another consideration is whether the analysts should interview as a team or work alone. Team interviewing can bring different perspectives to the questioning, provide a double check on what was said, and lead to productive postinterview discussions about what it all meant and whether the subject was reliable. Team interviewing can also yield a collection of complementary information. In one team interviewing project, it was striking to see two skilled interviewers, coming from seemingly the same perspective, taking quite different notes on the same interviews. The data collected were not in conflict, but what was thought to be important (and worth noting) was quite different. By combining notes, the analysts had a lot more information. Finally, team interviewing can provide support for novices who, if working by themselves, might be intimidated by the subject's attitude, style, or position.

Of course there are disadvantages to team interviewing. The evaluation team can meet with many more people if each analyst works alone. Subjects can feel outnumbered and ganged-up-on when faced by more than one outsider. Nevertheless, if time permits, team interviewing is probably preferable.

Getting Appointments

The problem of arranging appointments with individuals is like the problem of gaining entry to an agency, discussed in Chapter 2. You are an evaluator and many potential subjects will view you as a threat. Nonetheless, appointments, even with busy officials, usually are relatively easy to arrange by a simple phone call if you are courteous and willing to meet at the convenience of the subject. This direct approach works most of the time. If you anticipate trouble, you might want to name-drop—"By the way, Johnny Jones asked me to send you his best"—in hopes the subject will not refuse a friend's friend.

Other times, you may encounter stalling, runarounds, roadblocks, or out-and-out refusals to submit to an interview. If you can't get the information from someone else, you need to work out special approaches for getting appointments. One approach is to exert influence by asking a policymaker involved with the study to call the recalcitrant subject or his boss, or ask a mutual friend or acquaintance to ask the subject to do the interview as a favor.

You might also use flattery. Without overdoing it, you might tell the potential subject, perhaps in a letter, that he had been chosen because he is reputed to know more about the program than anyone else. Another approach is the veiled threat. You might imply that the report's results without the subject's comments would put him and his program in a bad light. A final approach is sheer persistence. I once sat in front of a potential subject's office every day for a week until, sick of the sight of me, he consented to an interview. You might not have that kind of time, but you can persist through repeated phone calls, visits, or letters. Once you are inside the door, even aggressive, annoying tactics tend to be forgotten, if you are a skilled interviewer. If the approaches do not work, remember that the result—no interview—is important information. It might indicate a busy official who is not interested in the study, but more often it might signal that something is going on that requires detailed pursuit from other angles.

Selecting the Time

In setting up appointments, it is important to think about timing. Should the subject be interviewed early or late in the study? Should he be interviewed at any particular time of the day? Should the arrangements for an appointment be made at a particular time—far in advance, or soon before?

Although high-level officials usually should be contacted first, it often pays to start your interviewing with lower-level officials. The early interviews are mainly to gather basic information and get a feel for the program issues. This is best done with officials below the top because they're likely to have more time. High-level officials might be available for only one meeting and should be interviewed later on. By then you will know the important questions, can explore subtleties and test interpretations, and will know whether you are getting straight answers.

In scheduling an important interview, inquire about a good time of day to get the subject's undivided attention. Some people are most relaxed and talkative outside regular working hours. Others have slow periods during the day when distractions can be minimized, such as teachers' planning periods.

When you make contact to arrange appointments can also be significant. In Florida, for example, the staff evaluating school accountability purposely did not schedule appointments far in advance; Monday morning appointments were scheduled on Friday afternoon. As a result, department officials did not have the time to get together and come up with a uniform, public relations response. In many cases, such a strategy is unnecessary because officials are more than willing to speak their minds. In other cases, you have to schedule well in advance to find a place on the full calendars of top-level executives. But when program officials feel under siege, as in Florida, creative tactics may be required to get straightforward answers.

Picking the Place

The ideal location for many interviews is a quiet, private place where the subject feels at ease. The objective is for the subject to focus exclusively on the substance of the interview, not on the surroundings. However, if recall of a certain event is your goal, it can help to conduct the interview where the episode occurred. For example, in trying to recollect the details of a school project, it can be useful to return to the school, walk the halls, visit classrooms, talk with project teachers, and generally see and hear things at the site that might act as reminders.

It's a good idea to visit subjects on their own turf. For one thing, they will often talk more freely in their own environment than in the evaluator's office. In Florida, for example, when staff members of the House Education Committee interviewed school officials as part of an evaluation, the staff purposely went to the schools where the educators worked. The chairman explains why:

[83]

> Teachers and school administrators will talk very freely, but if
> you get them in an environment that is the least bit in-
> stitutionalized, away from their own institution, it is very
> difficult to get open communication.[3]

Moreover, observing subjects in their daily work environments can
provide clues about how busy they are, their interpersonal relationships, their working conditions, and the climate of the work place.
All of this helps provide an accurate sense of what the program is
like in operation.

Sometimes, however, it pays to talk with officials away from
their own institutions, away from their busy offices and the hassles
of administration. Revealing data can be collected while munching
french fries at McDonald's, in a car on the way to a site, over a
drink at a hotel bar, or on a stroll around the park.

But interviewers can get carried away, as illustrated by the story
of a persistent journalist who tracked a reluctant Hubert Humphrey
to an amusement park. "How about doing an interview on the
roller coaster?" asked the reporter. "Fine," said Humphrey. As the
cars moved up an incline toward a plunge, the reporter asked:
"Senator, how does it look in terms of getting a big labor vote?"

"Well, Paul," began the senator, taking a look over the side,
"EEEEEYYYAAAAAAAHHHHHHH!!!"

"About the labor vote," persisted the reporter.

"Well," said Humphrey, heading for another plunge,
"YYYAAAAAAAHHHHHHH!!!" A petrified Humphrey was
speechless.[4]

Doing Homework

You need to do three types of homework before conducting
interviews. The substantive preparation is to learn about the program and the person to be interviewed. As part of the initial
scouting, start a list of specific questions that you will ask during
the interview. Whether these questions are typed on index cards or

jotted on the backs of envelopes is less important than getting in the habit of doing it. Learn enough about the program to know the answers to some of the questions you will ask. Also, learn whether there is anything special or peculiar about the subject that might affect the interview.

With this homework completed, you will be able to put what is said in context, make some sense out of it, and assess the accuracy of information obtained by comparing it with known data. What's more, a prepared interviewer will not annoy busy people with his ignorance. This emphasis on homework, of course, does not preclude the use of the interview as an exploratory device to discover important issues.

The second kind of homework focuses on your interviewing skills. If your evaluation project is staffed by a team, spend some time training. Take turns simulating interviews with difficult subjects. Practice asking different questions. Discuss how your skills could be improved. This training is especially important for novices who are nervous about their first interviews.

Finally, just as athletes get "up" for an important sporting event, you need to prepare yourself mentally for the interview. This entails a conscious effort to imagine how you would feel if you were the subject. What would your needs be and how could they be met? It also entails reflection on your role as interviewer. Your tasks involve detachment, skepticism and suspension of preconceptions—stances that might be different from those demanded when you are not conducting an evaluation. Interviewing requires concentration, sympathetic understanding, empathy, and a willingness to listen even if the material is boring or repetitious. If you are not "up," your interview will suffer.

Recording the Data

Before starting the interviews, still another decision has to be made—how to record what is said accurately and efficiently without the recording process inhibiting what is said. Various analysts hold strong and different opinions about this. Some interviewers just listen, not recording anything until immediately after the interview. Others, pencil and pad in hand, take detailed notes throughout the interview. Others rely on tape recorders, contending they could not interview without them. And still others use all three approaches, depending on the situation.

Obviously, each approach has its advantages and disadvantages. Delaying note-taking until after the interview assures that the subject will not be distracted by pencil scratchings or the presence of a microphone, and so the subject may speak more freely. But unless you have a faultless memory, quotations and other important information will be forgotten. Although this is a serious drawback, there are times when this approach is needed. For example, if you unexpectedly meet someone in the hall and start a conversation, you might sour the encounter by pulling out a pad or a recorder. Listen now, paraphrase later.

Copious note-taking during the interview means that quotations and key points can be recorded as they are made, thus avoiding the problem of recall. And by concentrating on those things that are important, you produce the edited record at the end of the interview, not after the hours of transcription required when you tape-record. Also, note-taking comes across as less serious and formal than tape recording. Subjects normally expect note-taking and thus it seems that they are not put off by it.

The disadvantages are that it is impossible to take everything down on paper; it is difficult to both listen carefully and record accurately; you can lose control of the interview by asking bad questions while listening, writing, and digesting; the subject can become fixated on your scribbling; and note-taking does not provide indisputable evidence of what was said, if someone claims he has been misquoted. Some of these problems can be solved by interviewing in teams with one person taking notes while the other asks the questions.

Tape-recording's obvious strength is that it provides an exact recording of what was said, that is, if your recorder is working, the mike is in the right place, and background noise doesn't drown out the interview. It is reassuring to have tapes to refer to when quotations are challenged. Indeed, some public officials, to avoid misquotes, demand that their interviews be recorded and that they receive a copy of the tape. Also, taped sessions allow the analyst to concentrate more on the interview, to ask better questions and to probe more effectively. Recorders are also useful when note-taking is impossible—for example, if you are interviewing during lunch. And recorders are a big help if you want to take down a quotation from a document, discovered at the interview site, that you can't quickly copy or take with you.

On the other hand, many analysts believe that most subjects clam up in the presence of a tape recorder because people are threatened by a verbatim transcript that might be used against them. In fact, some subjects will not even allow a recorder to be present in the room. Also, using a recorder can be prohibitively expensive. According to one estimate, it takes roughly nine hours for a typist to transcribe each hour of tape.[5] And you can spend an enormous amount of time going over the tapes and the transcripts.

You should weigh the advantages and disadvantages of each approach to collecting data and experiment with all three approaches if resources permit. If tape recording is impossible because of its costs, a middle ground might be to take notes on most of the interviews, record the most important ones, and use the recorder to tape interview notes (which will be discussed later). In the end, the method used should be the one that fits the circumstances, is affordable, and is comfortable for the parties to the interview.

II. SETTING THE TONE

"Judge a man by his questions rather than by his answers," Voltaire said. He may have been right in general, but in interviewing, good questions can fall flat unless you establish a good working relationship with the subject, one that is open and relaxed, and marked by trust and rapport. In this section, I examine how this is done in the crucial first stages of the interview, and how this relationship can be maintained. The tactics discussed can make a big difference, but they also very quickly can become contrived because it is hard to fake curiosity and sincere interest. What's probably the best advice should be obvious: Treat all subjects, regardless of their rank, as unique human beings who have something important to say.

Introduction

The first thing the subject hears is your introduction. Politely explain who you are, who you represent, why the subject was chosen, and the purpose of the study.

> How do you do, Mr. Smith. My name is Tom Parker. I'm an analyst with Senator Brown's Subcommittee on Special Education which, as you probably know, is reviewing the state's programs for handicapped children. I very much appreciate your willingness to meet with me. Senator Brown wanted me to get your views because of your knowledge of the program. I have a few questions in your area of expertise. Your statements will be regarded as strictly confidential.

Note the succinct description of the evaluation's purposes. In most cases, subjects want only a rough idea of the study's goals, not a lengthy explanation of all the objectives and underlying hypotheses. The statement of appreciation and the bit of flattery are common courtesies. The subject will also appreciate knowing that he'll be capable of answering the questions and that the information will be handled with discretion and without distortion. Even if you spoke with the subject previously in setting up the interview, you'll want to say enough now to be clear about your purpose.

Confidentiality is a particularly important assurance. It is meant to protect the legitimate right of sources, and is sometimes required to get information. In program evaluation, most individuals are usually promised confidentiality, which means that they can be quoted in the final report but not by name. Quotations are attributed to a "staffer," "a recognized expert," or other suitable labels. The attribution ought to be specific enough to have some meaning, but vague enough to protect the subject's identity. However, if a subject will discuss a topic only "off the record" or "for background only," the material cannot be quoted at all.

In addition, confidentiality means that no one outsde the evaluation team will be told what the subject said. Some subjects appreciate specific assurance that their statements won't be shared with their bosses or appear in tomorrow's newspapers. Some important exceptions are an agency head, a program director, and a project spokesman, who by virtue of their positions and responsibility often are not promised confidentiality and who expect to be quoted by name.

As a practical matter, analysts sometimes don't mention confidentiality with subjects who know the rules of the game. They know their identities will be protected unless they are spokespeople. (If you're not sure, check back before using a subject's name in a report.) In some cases, if you think there's a chance that the material might be sought legally, for example by a subpoena, you might add to your statement about confidentiality, "except as required by law."* Generally, just mention the specific assurance and be prepared to discuss the precise meaning of confidentiality if the subject raises the issue.

Commonalities

During the first part of the interview, the objectives are not only to share information and to establish trust, but to put the subject at ease and to make a good personal impression. If the subject is

* The legal issues involving promises of confidentiality are discussed in Chapter 2.

relaxed and likes you, he may speak more candidly; people tend to respond to people they think are "okay." One way to facilitate this rapport is to establish commonalities before getting down to business. You might identify some common friends, geographical roots, career patterns, or distant relatives. For example, I once observed a half-hour "negotiation" over the rental of a building which was not really for rent. The discussion focused on mutual friends who had worked for the New York City subway system and on how the system had changed. Business was raised only at the last minute—in an instant a deal was struck. Here the renter combined good tactics with a genuine interest in mutual friends, and succeeded.

However, depending on the subject, such pleasantries may be unnecessary—and waste valuable time. Many subjects, particularly if they are high-placed and busy ones, want to get down to business immediately, get the interview over with, and move on to their next appointment.

Attitudes

With a good first impression, you're off to a good start. To maintain a good working relationship and motivate the subject to continue, be an attentive, sympathetic listener. You can convey this attitude by maintaining eye contact, ignoring distractions, asking appropriate follow-up questions, providing nonverbal responses, and verbal reinforcement. All this can signal to the subject that you are paying close attention, trying earnestly to understand his views, and taking what he says quite seriously. This can motivate subjects to continue talking because people in general encounter few good listeners.

You should also come across as nonjudgmental, as someone who is not evaluating the worth of what is being discussed. For example, don't say, "So you neglected to submit the report on time. Could you explain this failure?" Instead, say, "So the report was submitted late. Could you say more about the reason?" Be nonjudgmental also in your behavior (facial expressions, gestures, posture) and in response to questions from the subject. For example, it is not unusual for a subject to say, "What do you think about that?" A good response is, "I haven't formed an opinion. Right now I'm just trying to understand the views of the different parties." Or, "I'd be happy to discuss my developing views at the end of the interview. But now I'd like to protect the time so that I can fully understand your views." An interviewer who is judgmental can easily inhibit the subject from expressing his real attitudes or stating anything that might be embarrassing. Also, expressing opinions or taking sides can derail the conversation and divert it to your particular views—the more you talk, the less time for the subject.

Finally, be sincerely appreciative of the subject's time and effort. After all, answering questions can be hard work, and time spent in an interview could be spent elsewhere. The subject deserves a genuine thank you and other expressions of appreciation. For example, you might say, "I realize it's difficult to reconstruct what happened eight years ago when the law was passed, but I'd greatly appreciate it if you would try." Such expressions can help establish and maintain good relations, and open up the possibility of follow-up interviews.

III. Asking Good Questions

Good questions are ordered, worded, and asked so that they provoke the subject to respond honestly and completely, often going beyond what he intended to say. They are translations of the central evaluation questions. They elicit good quotes, revealing anecdotes and quality information about the substance of the program as well as the subject's background and frame of reference. The analyst who asks good questions can stimulate the subject to really think about the responses and to prolong the interview.

First Questions

First questions, like first impressions, can have a lasting effect. Consequently, they should be planned with care, and designed to fit the situation and the subject.

Usually, it makes sense to start off with easy, nonthreatening questions; throw your slow ball, not your strikeout sizzler. The question might focus on something the subject knows a lot about, for instance, how his program works. Or you might discard your planned opener and pick up on something overheard immediately before the interview. "As I came in, I couldn't help but hear you talking with your assistant about a workshop you are planning. Could you tell me about that?" With the first questions, the purpose is less to dig for information than to relax the subject and ease him into the rhythm of being interrogated. If the subject is comfortable with the questions and can answer without embarrassment, he will develop confidence that he has something to say. This approach is particularly important with those not in the habit of being interviewed.

Besides asking nonthreatening openers, you need to think about whether these questions should be broad or narrow in scope. In intensive interviewing, the first questions are by design typically wide open, vague, and ambiguous. "Would you start by describing your program?" "Could you begin by giving me some background on this school district?" Such questions provide the subject with room to answer in any way that suits him; embarrassing or threatening material can be avoided. In the process, the subject applies his own frame of reference to the question, often presenting information that might never come to light without the broad question's license to wander. You are also introduced to what the subject views as the salient issues. Thus, the broad question is often the ideal exploratory tool.

But it also has its problems. Some subjects are threatened by the lack of clear direction and by not knowing whether their responses are appropriate. This problem can be alleviated in part by providing the subject with cues that he is on target. Second, the subject might be annoyed, silently accusing you of asking questions that are answered in available documents. Avoid this by telling the subject that his perspective is of particular interest. Third, broad or vague openers can be quite boring, hardly the way to start with an uncooperative subject.

Because of these problems, some interviewers like to start with narrow questions. For example, if the subject is busy, constantly interviewed, or particularly nervous, you might show that you have done your homework, trying to capture the subject's attention as well as easing into the material. One interviewer started a session with a preoccupied President Kennedy by asking whether he was a "generation chauvinist" because JFK's calendar showed that most of his appointments were with people within a few years of his own age. Another started a session with Barbra Streisand by asking how she chose a nursery school for her son Jason.[6] These narrow openers were winners and both subjects were immediately hooked.

Other narrow openers are more mundane, but to the point. "Who are the key agency officials responsible for administering this program?" "What are your specific duties?" "What are the procedures for applying for funds?" Narrow questions, designed to elicit specific information, can start some subjects talking.

Both broad and narrow openers can be quite useful. One determining factor might be the stage of the evaluation. In early interviews, when the evaluation is more exploratory, broad openers can be particularly helpful in uncovering unknown issues. By contrast, toward the end of interviewing when you are closing in on the data, filling gaps, and tentatively testing hunches, narrow openers (as well as follow-ups) can nail down details and corroborate data.

Coping With Problems

After the preliminaries and during the serious questioning, you will typically encounter some difficulties in getting accurate, relevant, and reasonably complete information. Careful formulation of questions can alleviate many problems.

As an analyst, word your questions so the subject doesn't misunderstand or misinterpret them. Fortunately, because intensive interviewing is flexible, you can make corrections as you go along. You can often detect misunderstood questions by listening carefully to the answers, and clear up the matter in follow-up discussion.

But, generally, in questions intended to evoke clear, specific responses, use language that is simple and straightforward. The words should be part of the shared, everyday vocabulary of the analyst and the subject, rather than the jargon of the analyst's professional background.

Be certain that commonly shared words are commonly defined. For example, the meaning of "informant" to an anthropologist is different from the word's meaning to a typical lay person. It is appropriate to define words as part of a question. Shared meanings can also be achieved by adding sentences to the question that place the term in context or by asking the subject to define the term.

Also, remember that your frame of reference may be different from your subject's. This problem can be solved by incorporating your frame of reference into the question ("as compared with . . .") or by following the subject's response with the question, "Why?"

Avoid loaded words. "What is the impact of state monitoring on your program?" is a neutral question. Contrast that to "How do you feel about state bureaucrats snooping around your turf?" Also avoid multipart questions. You want your subject to concentrate on his response, not on the different parts of the question, how they relate, and what should be answered first. A double-barrelled question also makes it easy for the subject to avoid answering all of it by focusing on a thread and digressing.

Other problems arise, as discussed in Chapter 3, because the subject is unwilling to cooperate. If this is the case, and it seems that he thinks his responses might be embarrassing or thought to be in bad taste, you might word the question so that it sanctions the material. For example, a program officer may be hesitant to discuss the evolving character and hectic pace of his program because he believes it should be more orderly and rational. To encourage him to talk about the process, you might say, "There's lots of evidence that some good programs rapidly change their goals and practices as they go along. How about yours?" Alternatively, you might share intimacies with the subject or implicate yourself in the supposed offense. "When I operated a program like yours, I ran into a lot of messy problems and kept changing the program and its goals. Have you had similar experiences?" With this method, beware of putting words in the subject's mouth. Answers to leading questions need careful checking out.

Second, a subject may be unwilling to answer because of norms and traditions. Honest answers might violate unwritten rules that prohibit the discussion of interpersonal problems or politics, or acting discourteous to outsiders, even evaluators. In response, you might use the bandwagon approach. For example, you might say, "All organizations have to deal with problems of interpersonal conflict. How does your unit deal with its interpersonal problems?" Or, "I know from discussions with others that there have been some debilitating personal battles in this agency. Could you give me your perspective?" The hope is that the subject will break the rules because others have done so.

Another tactic is to demonstrate that a harsh response to you would not violate the norm of courtesy. For example, if you wanted the subject to engage you in a spirited debate, you might criticize some of your own earlier questions. This might encourage the subject to vent his own feelings without feeling impolite. Another approach is to acknowledge the subject's expertise or special knowledge in the hope that flattery will overcome his disinclination to break the rules. "You, Mr. Jones, are the only person here with a broad perspective on the program. Could you tell me how it evolved, and the ways in which politics were involved?"

A third problem of unwillingness develops when the subject perceives that his privacy is being invaded and as a matter of principle he will not cooperate. In response, it sometimes helps to acknowledge the problem straightforwardly, then continue. You might say, "Fine, can I reword the question, or is there part of it that you feel free to answer?" Or you might appeal for help, "If you think the next question is an invasion of privacy, don't feel compelled to answer, but we really need your perspective. . . ." This one-two punch might get an answer or it might justify silence because the subject did not think his privacy was being invaded until you told him. None of these tactics is foolproof, but sometimes they have to be tried because they might be the only way to loosen a tongue.

Even if the subject is willing, as is common, he may not be able to remember exactly what happened or the chronology. In such cases, you might be able to word the questions so that the subject is able to respond. Pose questions in a context that reminds him of some known facts: the date of the law's passage, where a program was located, who was in charge, the prevailing mood, or what others were doing. Reminded of the context, the subject may be stimulated to remember more. Another approach is to seek recognition rather than recall. For example, you might ask, "Which senator do you remember as being particularly influential at the time? Senator Able, Bond, or Grady?" "Do you remember where the idea for the task force came from? Was it from Bill Birch, Joan Moore, or perhaps Mary Peters?" In these cases, it helps if you know the answer you are trying to corroborate with the question.

Another approach is to ask the subject not about a specific issue but about what was generally happening to him and his organization at the time. For example, you might say, "In 1975, when the program was first started, what was your job and what was going on in the agency?" This discussion of associated events may jog his memory or alleviate confusion. A final approach is to ask questions designed to achieve a step-by-step reconstruction. If you have developed a tentative chronology from known facts and other accounts, you can often get a willing subject to corroborate facts and fill in blanks. In any case, the competent analyst is suspicious of retrospective data, particularly information touching on sensitive personal or program areas. He treats this information as in particular need of cross-checking and writes up reports on retrospective data with particular caution.

Probes

Intensive interviewing would be incomplete without the continual use of follow-up questions called *probes*, to dig for details and understanding. Four different kinds will be examined, and when and how they can be useful.

The first kind of probe is designed to evoke *clarification*. It is particularly useful when the subject has said something that is ambiguous, unintelligible, implausible, or inconsistent with an earlier part of the interview or with another account. The goal is to press the subject to state what he means in a way that is clear to you, even if it is an evasion or a lie. The probe itself might be nonverbal in the form of a squint, a frown, or a hand gesture. Or it can be verbal, such as "I don't understand." "If I understand you, you said . . . ." "I'm not quite clear on your point. Could you say a bit more?" The analyst might also summarize the subject's statements, saying, "To make sure that I've got you right, let me summarize your points . . . . Is that accurate?" In asking for clarification, it is usually more effective to portray the problem as your failure to understand, rather than as the subject's failure to communicate,—even if this is untrue. Little is to be gained by making the subject feel stupid or defensive.

A second kind of probe is designed to encourage *elaboration*. Here the subject has made an important point clearly, but has stopped prematurely. The goal is to get him to talk more about the topic, to flesh out opinions, facts, and perceptions. Verbal probes are most common: "Please say more," "Could you expand on that?" Elaboration might focus on the "what, when, and where," but also on explanation: "Why do you think that happened?" "How did that come about?" Here, as with clarification probes, it is often useful to ask for specific examples to buttress the point: "That's quite interesting, could you give me an example?" "Where did you see that in practice?" Also, you might ask for specific evidence: "How could I convince my boss that that is true?" "What evidence do you have on that?"

A third kind of probe is designed to provide *encouragement*. The subject might be talking along, perhaps in answer to a broad, ambiguous question. An encouragement probe signals to the subject that he is on target, is being quite helpful and should continue. These signals can be given nonverbally in the form of a smile, nodding the head, or determined note-taking that indicates the importance of the subject's words. Verbally, the probe might take the form of "uh-huhs," "That's really fascinating," "You don't say." "I understand your point." Also, you might echo the subject's words: "A great success, that's really important." These cues can be overdone, but a more typical mistake is for the interviewer to be too stingy in providing encouragement. And without that positive reinforcement, the subject's interest and motivation may wane.

Of course, some probes are designed to evoke both clarification and elaboration while encouraging the subject to continue. For example, you might clarify and rephrase the subject's response, showing him that you were listening and understood. "You believe that the children in your class aren't receiving enough help." "You feel badly about the program's effectiveness." This approach can be quite effective, particularly in enabling subjects to discuss emotion-charged matters.

The fourth kind of probe, often underutilized, is the *silent* one. What should you do when the subject stops talking? The usual response is to fill the void immediately with another question. Often, however, it makes more sense to say nothing for a few seconds. The subject typically will start talking again, clarifying and elaborating, often saying things that would have been missed if you had jumped too quickly into the breach.

Packaging of Questions

It is not enough to devise and ask good questions. They need to be packaged to maximize the flow of information. One might start with broad questions and then ask progressively more narrow ones. This so-called funnel approach is popular among deductive thinkers, who like to proceed from the general to the specific. A second pattern is to start with narrow questions and step by step move on to broader ones. Sherlock Holmes was a champion of this so-called inverted-funnel approach. The exploration of a topic using the funnel approach, and interspersing probes with the primary questions, might proceed like this: broad question, response, probe, response, narrower question, response, probe, and so on, until the material on the topic, if not the interviewee, is exhausted.

In packaging questions for the entire interview, there is general agreement about the preferred placement of difficult questions. Start off with easy questions, broach the tough questions toward the middle, and finish up with some light questions and a pleasant discussion. This sequence is intended to raise the difficult issues at a time when the subject is most likely to address them, and to end the interview on a friendly note so you can return for more.

In practice, of course, funnels, inverted funnels, and strategic placement of difficult questions will be affected by factors beyond your control. Once again, you should be flexible and ready to follow the flow of the interview.

Interview Guide

It does little good to plan good questions and package them effectively if you end up forgetting them when facing the subject. The only thing worse than a bad question is no question at all. An

[99]

interview guide can help avoid this. I am not suggesting the structured format typically found in survey questionnaires— strictly sequenced questions, followed by alternative probes depending on the answers to the primary questions. Rather, list the key issues to be covered and write out important questions to get the wording right. This guide serves as a quick reference during the interview, to help ensure that all topics are covered and that sensitive issues are dealt with sensitively. A common guide is also especially useful if a team of analysts have split up responsibility for interviewing different individuals and want to be sure that the same topics are covered.

Interview guides are not foolproof, of course. I once started an important session, guide in my lap, with a seemingly harmless question. The subject squinted and asked to see my questions. Flustered, I gave him my guide, which contained quickly-jotted notes prepared with no thought of sharing them. He liked the questions in my guide even less than my first question, got up, and threw me out of his office.

IV. ASKING CHALLENGING QUESTIONS

Sometimes, questions politely asked in a nonjudgmental and nonargumentative way do not elicit the data possessed by the subject and needed for the study. The subject might not take the interview seriously, or he might lie, evade the issues, or present a front. Or he may need further stimulation to jog his memory and capture his interest. In such cases, it is sometimes appropriate to resort to more challenging, determined questioning. The skilled analyst asks challenging questions only after weighing the risks. In no case, does it make sense to just get frustrated and bow out.

There are many different types of questions to challenge the subject to say more than he intended or thought he knew. The seven varieties listed might stimulate you to think of others. At the same time, you must keep in mind several caveats. Challenging questions may anger the subject, or they may lead the subject to erroneously agree with an answer that you seem to prefer simply to satisfy you. The latter is less of a problem with government officials who are used to defending their positions than with those not normally interviewed. Also, in using information gathered in other interviews as the basis for a question, remember to protect the confidentiality promised other subjects. And, of course, how a question is asked can be as important as what is asked.

To the Core, Matter of Factly

Sometimes the best approach is the direct approach—ask the challenging question and don't make a big deal about it being a big deal. Direct, challenging questions can ask for sensitive information, confront the subject with inconsistencies, and lead the subject in a particular direction. Some examples include: "Is it true that you have opposed the program from its beginning?" "What were the differences between the position taken by your agency and by the budget office?" "Your statement just now contradicts what you said publicly last year. How do you account for the difference?" "Isn't it true that the decision to fund was made on political grounds?" "What you've said doesn't make sense for these reasons. . . . What's your view?" Direct questions need not be hostile, and they often are quite appropriate for individuals accustomed to arguing their case and comfortable with confrontation.

Pointing to Someone Else

Suppose that the problem is to get information about a particularly sensitive area and you don't think direct confrontation will work. One way to motivate the subject, while softening the question, is to attribute the question to someone else (or group), even if you agree with its underlying premise. "As you know, Mr. Commissioner, your department has a widespread reputation in the legislature of being poorly managed. I wanted to give you this opportunity to rebut that charge." "The press has held you responsible for the program's not working. What is your response to these charges?" "As you know, your critics claim that you haven't been very aggressive with your local counterparts. I want to ask you to respond to your critics." These "some people say" observations can be effective introductions to difficult questions.

Devil's Advocate

You can also disassociate yourself from a challenging question by playing the role of devil's advocate, perhaps relying on evidence gathered elsewhere during the study. For example, the question might go like this: "Mr. Johnson, I really think that's a helpful answer, but let me play the devil's advocate for just a moment. The practices that you described as impossible seem to be in operation in five school districts in this state. Can you say more about why the state cannot expand these practices?" Without the introductory remarks, the questions might quickly anger or threaten the subject because they contradict him.

Raising the Sail, Lowering the Boom

Still another way to soften a challenging question is to balance what the subject might view as criticism with some praise. "According to a lot of people, you have done a remarkable job in dealing with the cities. But how much effort has gone into your dealings with rural areas?" "I've talked to a number of legislators who are really pleased with the job you are doing. But one of the things that concerns me is the level of effort that has gone into this project. Could you talk about that?" A subject who is happy with the praise and feeling confident will often be willing to talk about problem areas.

"What-If"

Suppose the subject has responded to the questions and probes, but you still are dissatisfied with the answer because it is incomplete, or it doesn't specify the reasons. Or suppose you are considering a recommendation for the program and you want some preliminary feedback. In both these cases, "what-if," or hypothetical questions, can come in handy. "Hm, that's interesting. But what would have happened if the legislature hadn't adopted the amendments? How would things have been different?" "What would have happened if the current staff had come on board earlier?" "What would happen if the legislature required stricter standards?" "What would happen if the program were abolished?" This last question, in particular, has a way of motivating even taciturn agency officials.

Creating an Image

A related follow-up to incomplete answers is to present an imaginary picture of the program and ask the subject how things might have been different. For example, you might pose the ideal. "Suppose the legislature had appropriated money on time, and you could have hired people without Civil Service clearance. Comparing that with reality, how would things have been different?" Or you might pose conditions worse than existed. "Just for the sake of argument, let's suppose that when the program started, no one knew anything about retarded children and that your staff was half its size. In what ways would the results have been worse?"

A variant on this is to ask the subject himself to pose the ideal or worst case, then discuss how things would have been different. "Suppose you could exercise your will over the legislature. What would you recommend, and how would it make a difference?" "Imagine that you had a chance to initiate the program again. What would you have done differently?" "Suppose you had been an opponent of the program in its early days. What could have been done to undermine its impact?" Such comparisons, imaginary situations, and role-playing can work if the subject is "into" the interview and intrigued by the questions. They can also lead to "I'd rather answer questions dealing with reality."

Offering a Version

Another way to cope with an uncooperative subject is to offer your own tentative version of what happened, why it happened or what it means, then ask the subject to give his assessment. "I've been trying to figure out how the decision was made to open the new hospital. The picture I've pieced together is this. . . . How does that square with your recollection?" "One of the things I've learned from examining this program is. . . . Do you agree with that interpretation?" "After five days of interviewing, I think I understand why the project wasn't fully implemented. . . . How does that explanation strike you?" These kinds of laying-your-cards-on-the-table questions can lead to various responses. The best one, from a weary interviewer's perspective, is for the knowledgeable subject to corroborate your version, and perhaps even add some supporting details. Another possible response is for the subject to express surprise: "I've never quite thought about it that way." A third response is for the subject to tell you that you are all wet. "But why?" is the rejoinder that might lead to new information. On the other hand, if your interpretation strikes the subject as preposterous or grossly unfair, it might lead you to the door.

V. FINISHING UP

It is useful to end an intensive interview like a soap opera, by not really ending it. Leave open the possibility to continue the discussion, either by phone or in person. When the subject shows signs of restlessness, you might say, "I know you're really tied up today, so why don't we call it quits. Maybe we can get back together sometime soon. Okay?" The hope is that the subject will feel obliged to continue later, after you have puzzled over what he has said and devised some good follow-up questions and tactics.

In addition to preparing for a return visit, you also want to elicit suggestions for further interviews and further issues to cover. "Who else should I talk to for a complete picture of the program?" "If I wanted a different perspective from yours, who would be a good person to see?" "How familiar would the commissioner be with the details of what we've been talking about? Should I see him?" These questions will help make sure that important issues are covered, that an array of people are contacted, and that the interview ends on an inoffensive note.

With the final questions answered, thank the subject for his time, effort, and answers, but avoid leaving too quickly. With the pencil put away (or the recorder off) and the official interview over, subjects frequently will relax and open up. If this happens, keep the talk going, make a mental note of those barriers that might have inhibited earlier communication and remember the new material. Postinterview chitchat can be quite revealing.

Interview Notes

After you leave, the next step is to go over your notes, if you used pad and pencil. Normally, I make a beeline for a quiet place (an empty office, a park bench, my car, the men's room), sit down and start writing.

You should fill in the blanks, spell out abbreviations, and generally make things legible and intelligible. The interview typically moves faster than the pencil, and shortcuts understood today can be gibberish tomorrow. Moreover, it is important to clearly mark those statements that are direct quotations so they can be identified for proper use in the final report. Finally, it is important to write down (or tape-record) what took place in the postinterview session. If you can remember exact quotations, all the better. If not, get the gist of what was said, including anecdotes. Later, as part of your field notes (see Chapter 5), you can record your reflections on the overall interview experience.

Final Steps

With the interview over and your notes in hand, three things remain to be done. One is to follow up the interview with a brief thank-you note, a simple courtesy that can help to keep open the relationship with the subject. The second is to make sure that your interview notes or tapes are carefully stored so that promised confidentiality will not be breached.

The last follow-up task is to compare information from the recent interview with other interview data and information collected by other techniques. How it fits with other material will point to necessary next steps in the data collection process.

VI. CONCLUDING COMMENT

Good interviewing is not easy. Before you begin, you must make crucial choices about the suitability of the method, who should be interviewed, when, where, and why. You must line up appointments, and prepare both substantively and mentally for the process. You must prepare at least a partial list of important issues to be covered. During the interview, you must repeatedly diagnose the situation, listening and looking for signs of lack of comprehension, reactions to your presence, unwillingness, and inability. You must constantly monitor your own behavior, biases and shortcomings, and reactions to the subject. Based on this, you must make on-the-spot judgments about how to act, what to say, the direction to take, and when to stop. You must formulate a provocative question, listen carefully to the answer, evaluate its validity and relevance, record the answer, and provide nonverbal cues. Then you must anticipate the next question, shape it in your mind, think about what has yet to be covered, consider challenging the subject, remember the question being answered, remember what has been covered, then start all over again as the interview shifts to a new topic. While all this is going on, you must keep the subject motivated, on target, and honest—without coming across as a nervous wreck.

It is not far off the mark to suggest that ideal interviewers are those who combine the skepticism of the Apostle Thomas, the investigative instinct of Jack Anderson, the dogged persistence of Billie Jean King, the warmth of Bing Crosby, the quarterbacking skills of Joe Namath, and the unsullied integrity of Queen Elizabeth. It is these traits, combined with a probing intellect, good intuition, flexibility, and luck, rather than a rigid adherence to "how-to" techniques, that are crucial in gathering accurate, relevant, and reasonably complete information. To be sure, if I knew any interviewers who possessed all these traits, I would have asked them to write this chapter.

5

Transient Observation and Document Analysis

INTENSIVE INTERVIEWING, the principal fieldwork method used in evaluating social programs, has its limitations, as do other methods. In addition, coping with bias and error requires the use of more than just a single method. Two other data collection techniques, transient observation and document analysis, are essential complements to intensive interviewing. They can uncover new information and corroborate other data, as each technique compensates for the weakness of the others.

I. TRANSIENT OBSERVATION

Defining Terms

Before discussing the what and how of *transient* observation, it is important to distinguish it from *participant* observation, the term normally linked with long-term qualitative research and some kinds of field evaluations. Essentially, observational studies differ along three dimensions: whether the subjects know that they are being observed; the length of observation time; and the status of the observer within the group—full-fledged member, quasi member, or outsider.

Participant observation   This term is usually associated with the work of anthropologists and sociologists who with permission enter an organization, group, or society to collect data. While there, the researcher participates in the day-to-day living of his subjects, then leaves to analyze his observations, carefully recorded in field notes. A study of one site might take several years. (A variant on this is the full-fledged member of a group—for example, a school principal—who decides to also become an observer and announces his intentions.)

This sustained immersion in group activities allows the analyst to build trust, to overcome reactions to his presence, to observe a range of activities and, in the process, to gain an excellent, firsthand knowledge of what is happening and why. It would be an ideal observational role for the program evaluator addressed in this book were it not for the extraordinary costs in time.[1]

Transient observation   As defined here, the transient observer observes without disguise, is clearly an outsider, and, is faced with tight time constraints. Unable to actively participate in the life of the program and observe day-to-day activities, the transient observer uses all his senses as he interviews subjects, attends meetings, roams the halls, and generally hangs around. While the subjects usually know when they are being observed, the transient observer might also be an unannounced observer at a large meeting, or on occasion an unnoticed observer of a passing remark heard around the corner. On a two- to three-day visit to a site, perhaps a fifth of the time would be spent in transient observations outside the interviews.[2]

Advantages and Limitations

The first question is why conduct transient observation at all? The method has severe limitations. You obviously can't observe things in the past or be in more than one place at a time to observe current program activities. And observing, like interviewing, is usually subject to the Hawthorne effect and other sources of bias, such as your limitations as an observer. These problems are exacerbated because a transient observer has little time to develop trust and become a part of the woodwork. Also, it is easy to misinterpret observed behavior if you don't ask subjects about its meaning. Finally, observation can turn out to be quite inefficient. You might observe for days but not see anything important.

Despite these limitations, transient observation has several advantages. If you want to know what actually is occurring, there is no better way to find out than to observe it yourself, rather than rely on the potentially unreliable reports of others. Observation also allows you to collect data that you might not even know to ask about in an interview or that would not be reported (nonverbal behavior, taken-for-granted activities, routine operations). Finally, direct observation can play an important role in cross-checking your data. What someone says can be compared with what he does, or his opinions of what is generally happening can be corroborated. If the subject is a good reporter about current activities, corroborated through observation, he may be a reliable reporter about past activities.

What to Observe

The specific things observed by the transient observer will depend largely on the subject of the evaluation and the issues being examined. If you were evaluating an education program for handicapped children, one thing you might observe is professional interaction in meetings evaluating individual children. If you were studying parental involvement in the schools, you might look for signs of school administrator dominance in parent-council meetings. If you were examining hospital-community relations, you might focus on the care of the poor in hospital emergency rooms.

Regardless of the content of the particular evaluation, the

analyst should observe in the following six areas. In any one of them, you might discover something new, corroborate interviews, or pick up cues that suggest further investigation.

Individual characteristics The sex, race, age, profession, dress, and appearance of the individual being interviewed or the group being observed can give significant clues. For example, if white professionals dominate a conference on urban poverty, there may be a major problem. If key officials fail to attend a meeting, the meeting may be only symbolic. A large turnout at a rally for the elderly might verify statements about their political participation. In the beginning of an evaluation, such characteristics should be observed and recorded. Later they can be interpreted and verified; they might mean what you originally thought, or something entirely different.

Interactions By observing people interact, you might get an idea of power relationships, decision-making processes, current issues, pressing crises, management styles, important actors, standard procedures, attitudes toward clients and agencies, levels of enthusiasm, general climate, and the like. Interactions can be observed during interviews. When a subject is interrupted by a phone call or by another visitor, you have an opportunity to observe. Interactions can also be observed in meetings, conferences, rallies, hallways, outer offices, classrooms, parking lots, lounges, bars, and restaurants. For example, a spirited discussion of new policies over lunch could signal a cohesive group. If possible, record what you see and hear—quotes, loud voices, arguments, bored replies and all.

Nonverbal behavior You need not be an expert on nonverbal behavior to make use of some important clues. Just as poker players might watch for their opponents' pupils to widen as a sign of a good hand, you can learn to recognize a few facial expressions, gestures, body postures, and leg movements. Considered in the overall context of what the subject is saying and doing, nonverbal behavior can sometimes help you gauge whether he is ready and willing to cooperate. It can also lead to unwarranted conclusions if you are not careful.

For example, you might look for signs of boredom or disinterest: a yawn, a faraway stare, a turning away of the body or head, a slouched body, or glances at a clock. A feigned smile or too loud a laugh could suggest preoccupation with something else. As an interviewer, you can ignore these signals, switch to a more interesting topic, try to ask more provocative questions, or suggest that you finish at another time, because a bored subject might not provide complete answers.

You might also look for signs of nervousness. Sweating, blushing, and heavy breathing are particularly obvious, but leg and foot wiggling, crossing and recrossing of legs, darting eyes, and clenched fists might also be signs. A nervous subject might be influenced by the analyst's presence, and could be hiding something or unable to answer certain questions. Of course, the subject might just be a nervous person. In any case, you might respond by switching to less threatening questions, by changing the topic, or perhaps by confronting the subject directly about his anxiety.

Now, whether any of these nonverbal cues actually mean anything, is always hard to tell. It would be foolish, of course, to draw any conclusions from them alone. But they can signal that things don't quite fit, suggesting the need for further corroboration.[3]

Props   People surround themselves with props—books, photographs, special name plates, plaques, mementos, paintings, wall hangings, and posters. Such things dotting your subject's office can provide insight into his background, interests, values, attitudes, and intellectual leanings. The books on a subject's shelves might help explain why he espouses a particular set of solutions. A plaque might point to a lobby group with which he has special ties. A poster might suggest his political leanings.

Props also can provide a conversation piece. I once started an interview by asking about a photo on the subject's desk of a prize striped bass. A few minutes of story swapping about striper fishing provided a relaxed introduction to a serious interview.

Walls are perhaps the best place to find revealing props— newspaper clippings, cartoons, fliers, and sayings. While studying the impact of master planning on state government, I spotted the following notice on the office wall of a key advocate of planning:

NOTICE

THE OBJECTIVE OF ALL DEDICATED DEPARTMENT EMPLOYEES SHOULD BE TO THOROUGHLY ANALYZE ALL SITUATIONS, ANTICIPATE ALL PROBLEMS PRIOR TO THEIR OCCURRENCE, HAVE ANSWERS FOR THESE PROBLEMS, AND MOVE SWIFTLY TO SOLVE THESE PROBLEMS WHEN CALLED UPON. . . .

HOWEVER . . .

WHEN YOU ARE UP TO YOUR ASS IN ALLIGATORS, IT IS DIFFICULT TO REMIND YOURSELF THAT YOUR INITIAL OBJECTIVE WAS TO DRAIN THE SWAMP.[4]

Such props can lead to direct questions about the subject's real views.

In another official's office, I found the following story tacked to the wall:

> There is a tale concerning a man named Joe. Joe had the finest lamb in all Armenia, with the longest and softest fleece. The lamb was so famous that Joe's neighbors decided to steal it. When he saw them coming, Joe carried the lamb into his cabin and barred the door. He began shooting at the robbers, first from the window on the east, then from the window on the west, then from the east again. But each time Joe crossed the room, he tripped and fell over the lamb. Finally, he opened the door, kicked the lamb outside, and went on shooting.[5]

This official had portrayed himself in interviews as someone deeply concerned about overzealous bureaucrats forgetting the rationale for state rules and regulations. The saying on the wall, obviously not placed there for my consumption, provided some corroboration for the official's self-portrayal.

Physical surroundings   The setting in which a program operates can provide clues. For example, housing program staff in offices a block from central headquarters might suggest a low-priority program. A large office, located near the commissioner's, might indicate a high-status official. A bulletin board might suggest current issues and activities. Chipping paint could suggest a maintenance problem. Because such signals can be obvious, those indicating problems are typically removed before an official visit. Those that remain should be recorded and later interpreted.

Unobstrusive measures[6]   Less obvious signals of problems or performance are often overlooked by subjects who are sprucing up the setting for a visit. This type of inconspicuous evidence, called unobtrusive measures, can be quite useful because it is not affected by the analyst's questions or his presence—the Hawthorne effect is minimized.

These clues usually take the form of *physical remains* or *wear spots* and are familiar to us all. The tracker looks for footprints, broken twigs, and clumps of fur to stay on the animal's trail. The detective searches for fingerprints, car-oil drippings, and remnants of gun powder to identify a suspect. The horse trader checks for worn teeth to determine the mare's age. In program evaluation, similar clues exist even though they are typically overlooked for want of imagination. Underlining in the project director's copy of the regulations could signal that the law is taken seriously. Accumulated dust on state-purchased equipment might indicate waste. Coffee cups and cigarette butts might point to a tense meeting. The smudged pages and cracked spine of a book on a principal's desk might indicate its influence. Worn tiles in front of a museum exhibit might demonstrate its popularity. Sometimes the absence of even such inconspicuous evidence can be telling, too. The lack of graffiti in the restrooms or sparkling clean floors even in busy corridors might signal that "just another day in the life of the school" is an atypical day especially planned for you.

The Process of Observation

How you conduct your observations will depend in part on where you are observing. During an interview, you will observe the subject and his surroundings without making special arrangements or announcements about observing. Similarly, while roaming the halls, sitting in an office awaiting an appointment, or standing in the agency cafeteria line, you need not spotlight your casual observation. Or if you were part of a crowd at a hearing on a piece of legislation, you would have no need to announce your activities.

But when you are observing in a setting not typically open to the public—a classroom, a staff meeting, or an evaluation session on a handicapped child—you need to announce your presence and take steps to minimize bias and error. Doing this requires many of the same procedures as for interviews: a proper introduction, nonjudgmental manner, responsiveness to questions, appreciative attitude, and generally an attempt to establish trust, rapport, and a relaxed atmosphere. Just as the early part of an interview usually doesn't produce much useful data, neither do such observations. After a while, though, your presence may have less effect.

Besides considering the Hawthorne effect, it is important to take steps to deal with several other problems encountered in observational work. If you are on-site as part of an official visit, you will typically be given a tour of what the project director would like you to see. While it would be impolite to refuse the grand tour, it would be a mistake not to observe people and places at times different from those suggested by your guide. You might be able to do some wandering on your own, as well as get suggestions for additional observations from your subjects and informants. But there is a danger here. Because you can't be everywhere at once, your report might emphasize certain things just because you accidentally happened to observe them. Also, you might observe atypical behavior because of your timing; the day you visited a class was the day before a vacation or the day after a big examination. To deal with these problems, ask your subjects about what can't be overlooked and about the representativeness of the behavior. Also, if possible, sample behavior on a random basis over time.

In doing such observations, you will increasingly become more systematic, as you get deeper into the study. In the beginning, you might observe "everything" to help you get the overall flavor. Later, your observations will become more focused. And just as you develop an interview guide to help you remember important questions, you might develop a checklist of things to look for while observing.

Field Notes

It is one thing to observe and it is another to remember what you saw and heard. You must take steps to record your observations. Some of this can be done on the spot. For example, if you were attending a large school board meeting, taking notes probably would not distract those present. But on-the-spot jottings always need to be supplemented by field notes that provide an accurate, reasonably complete record of your observations.

Your field notes should be a detailed record of your observations supplementing your interview notes. Describe settings, activities, and people. Record quotes, paraphrases, and gists of conversations. Note individual characteristics, interactions, nonverbal behavior, physical surroundings, and unobtrusive measures. But field notes should go beyond simply what you saw. You will want to write up your tentative interpretations of what the data mean. What are their significance? What hunches do they suggest or support? How do they corroborate or contradict other data?

Finally, it is important to record your reactions to the data, your assessment of bias and error, and your evaluation of the safeguards used. How does the subject come across? Was he natural or reacting to my presence? Willing and able? Dull or inspiring? Ultimately, was what I saw and heard believable? Do the data have the ring of truth? Are the data on target? What more is needed? Are there major holes that still need filling? Did I hold my predispositions in check? How did I feel? What difference does that make? Am I the same observer I was when I started this project? What tactics worked?

One objective is to have on record enough rich detail so that later you will be able to recall not only what you saw and heard, but also the setting, context, specific details, and your tentative assessment of the data's significance. Another objective is to have a log of how your feelings and predispositions have changed so you can gauge their effect on your observations.

Of course, if you put all this detail in your field notes, you could easily end up with time for little else. In fact, in participant observation studies, it is not unusual for the writing of field notes to take one to three times as long as the observations themselves. That's impossible for the type of evaluation that this book emphasizes. A compromise is to quickly jot down some notes after your transient observations, then prepare more extensive notes back in the office or at night. As a rule of thumb, these condensed field notes might take a couple of hours for each day of fieldwork. Preparing even condensed field notes can be grueling work, but the more you delay, the more difficult the task and the more that is forgotten.[7]

In sum, be alert to physical and personal clues that can be garnered through transient observations. However, in using observational data remember that it is awfully easy to jump to erroneous conclusions. You need to question the meaning of what you saw, gauge the Hawthorne effect, cross-check your data with other methods, check the representativeness of your observations, look for omissions in your data, resist guided tours as your only source of data, and immediately record notes. With these precautions, observations can be among the best source of information because you collected the data directly.

II. Document Analysis

At this point, you might wonder why it is necessary to rely on still a third method for collecting data. Besides the importance of cross-checking and triangulating, are there other reasons to go beyond interviewing and observing? In fact, while document analysis has its limits, it also has many advantages worth exploiting over other methods.[8]

Advantages and Limitations

Document analysis is better than interviewing for collecting some kinds of retrospective data. A thorough reading of available material might fill important gaps in the data caused by your not knowing enough to ask all the right questions. For example, data on high turnover rates could indicate a management problem; data on low school attendance might signal a potential dropout problem. Also, interview data are always plagued by memory problems and the filtering of data through current norms. Documents written at the time (for example, newspaper articles) aren't subject to recall problems and do reflect the contemporary climate. They may also provide more detail on the chronology of events than you could get through interviewing alone. Moreover, document analysis provides data that you wouldn't be likely to discover through interviewing. For example, to demonstrate that the time spent on writing was decreasing in the schools, one researcher documented the declining sale of lined paper to the schools and increasing sale of ditto paper. Another researcher, demonstrating

Irish domination in the Boston public schools, identified Irish surnames on a list of employees.[9]

Document analysis is also the most efficient way to collect certain kinds of information. If you need general background material on a program (basic statistics, a list of key staff, lines of formal authority, perceived issues), it's far better to read available materials than to waste the time of busy officials. If you want to learn what the program says it is doing (the stated goals or the public presentation), documents are the ideal source. If you want to learn about professional opinion on program-related issues, read professional journals. If you need data from distant places, check for documents at your local library.

Documents also are a big help in convincing the reader of the credibility of your report. A statement of what you saw or heard is just not as convincing as a quote taken directly from an internal memorandum. In the reader's eye, such documents could counteract charges of analyst bias.

Documents might be the only source for some data. If a person is unwilling or unable to be interviewed, or if the organization is uncooperative, available documents might help fill the gap. Finally, documents are convenient to work with. You don't have to worry about getting appointments, establishing rapport, or making travel arrangements. You can work with them when you want and return to them as you please.

Despite all these advantages, documents also have severe limitations. First, they often are purposely misleading, designed to sell the program rather than to reveal its flaws. As one experienced analyst put it, "If I were forced to choose between the documents on the one hand, and late, limited, partial interviews with some of the principal participants on the other, I would be forced to discard the documents."[10] Fortunately, such a choice is usually not necessary.

Even if the document is not purposely misleading it might suffer from many of the same problems found in interviewing—after all, a document is simply a written report rather than an oral one. The

writer might have memory problems, be guided by predispositions, or be a poor observer. With a document, you can scribble
"why?" in the margin, but you cannot cross-examine. You cannot
size up the subject to make a judgment about his reliability as a
reporter.

Another limitation is that although reams of material may be
available, it often will not contain much of the needed information
or be sufficiently detailed. In Connecticut, for example, legislative
analysts conducting a student aid evaluation found piles of reports,
but they did not contain such crucial information as how 6,000
students were chosen for aid out of 30,000 applicants, or what
happened to those not receiving aid. If you are interested in internal
processes and decision-making procedures, such data will usually
not be available.

Because of these limitations, a document by itself is often
useless or suspect. It needs to be cross-checked with other documents written from different perspectives and the information
needs to be triangulated through other methods. However, because
of the advantages of document analysis, it ought to be exploited,
with care, in every program evaluation.

Kinds of Documents

As you dig for information, you will often discover a surprising
number of documents reflecting the different perspectives of different sources. The kinds of documents that should be examined
can be grouped into six overlapping categories.

Official program records   Every government program maintains
records and produces reports about its origin, history, operation,
and impact; these are an important source of documentary evidence. For one thing, they set forth the legal basis for the program.
You should collect copies of the law, rules, regulations,
guidelines, and legal interpretations. In addition, program docu-

ments (for example, annual reports, financial statements, program brochures, newsletters, budget justifications) provide general background material as well as project the images that officials would like others to view. These documents, prepared primarily for public consumption, are usually accurate on basic facts, but are uncritical of program practices.

Government programs also produce internal documents that reveal a lot about program inner workings—operational plans, organizational charts, staff reports, minutes of meetings, personnel actions, draft budget documents, evaluations, reorganization plans, and memoranda (the chief device for communicating government business). Memos are particularly useful in revealing pressing issues, the arguments behind different positions, and who stands where. Their distribution lists also indicate who seems to count in making particular decisions (and whom you should see for additional information). These internal documents usually portray program operations more realistically than public relations material.[11]

Finally, many programs maintain "case files" on individuals served by the program: welfare case files, patient records, individual education plans for handicapped children, consumer complaints. For example, a Connecticut evaluation of programs for handicapped children stated:

> This section is based upon a review of records maintained by both the referring agency and the PF [private facility]. . . . The major purposes in examining these 15 written records were to determine their completeness, and to make some value judgments relative to the appropriateness of a particular program for a particular child. Obviously, a written report is not a complete report of what is happening to or for the child, but. . . . it is the only permanent record available to a referring agency.[12]

If confidentiality is not breached, these case files can provide quite useful insights into how a program operates.

Other government reports   In addition to the bureau administering the program, other government units will have produced helpful information. These include other units in the executive branch (for example, the agency in which the program is housed, the central budget office, the audit agency, the governor's office), other branches of government (for example, the legislative appropriations committee, the courts), or other levels of government (for example, recipient agencies, federal agencies).

The documents might bear either directly or indirectly on the program. The annual reports and historical accounts of the agency that includes the program, or the speeches of top agency executives could help put the program in a broader context. Statistical reports from the Census Bureau could provide useful demographic data on the areas served by the program. Reports on similar programs administered by other agencies might add perspective to your consideration of the program being evaluated. Finally, and often most important, other agencies of government may have evaluated the program. An audit-agency report, a management review, a budget hearing transcript, or an oversight review report can all provide critical information.

An excerpt from a Connecticut compensatory education evaluation provides a specific example of the use of program records and other government documents:

> On these visits to [local school districts] we examined . . .
> project descriptions, program evaluations, application
> forms, newsletters, class lists, staff assignments documents, . . . In addition, we examined a variety of other material including data on compensatory education programs in other states, HEW audit reports, . . . [federal] regulations and guidelines, analyses of other compensatory education programs, and various other documents that held out the possibility of providing a helpful perspective on . . . [the program].[13]

To a program administrator, much of this documentation is needless reporting and red tape; to the analyst, government paperwork and reports are a rich source of data.

Outside reports Many individuals and groups, besides public agencies, produce and maintain documentary evidence about government programs. The most obvious are the media. But it would not be unusual if the program you are studying is not considered newsworthy or has not been covered since its initiation. Other sources include advocacy groups, parent councils, lobby groups, research institutes, and individuals with a particular interest in the program. The documents might take the form of newspaper articles, annual reports, evaluations, research analyses, dissertations, internal memoranda, and exchanges of correspondence. These unofficial documents provide a needed counterbalance to official documents.

Books and things Books, magazines, articles in professional journals, and other library material might give you some indirect help in doing the evaluation, particularly in thinking about recommendations. There are limits on how much literature review is possible, of course. But, for example, you might find up-to-date analyses of the issues faced by similar programs, helping you to put things in a broader context. You might get some hints on how to think about or organize your material by examining how others have handled similar material. You also can get access to recent professional opinion on what should be happening in the general area addressed by the program.

Personal records Individuals leave important documentary tracks that can enhance program evaluation. These documents include diaries, personal correspondence, notes on meetings, logs of telephone calls, appointment calendars, memos for the record, field notes, autobiographies, or scrapbooks. Officials often like to maintain their own records for posterity, not to mention for self-protection on sensitive matters. These materials are often unavailable, but if you can get access they can be invaluable in understanding an individual's perspective and in getting an unofficial view of what happened and why. Personal records can provide revealing contrasts to documents prepared for public consumption.

Audiovisual material   As we know from the Nixon tapes of the White House Oval Office, documentary evidence doesn't come just in the form of the written word. Tape recordings, slides, photographs, diagrams, plot plans, blueprints, models, drawings, cartoons, and charts all can provide important data. While working on a project examining the safety of fish processing plants, I came across some photographs of bug-infested work environments. These photos provided excellent documentation of unsanitary conditions.

Finding the Documents

Finding all these documents is not a leisurely, feet-on-the-desk operation. You need to ask, explore, and follow-up, just as you do in an interview.

Throughout the study, ask everyone you interview for documentary evidence about the program. Think of others who might have had a reason to commit something to paper. These sources include agency officials, informants, news reporters, advocacy group members, lobbyists, trade associations, professional organizations, legislative aides, program clients. For example, at the end of an interview ask: "What should I read to get a complete picture of the program?" "Did anyone ever evaluate the program?" "Who might have important documents that I should read?" Also, be explicit about internal documents and personal records. "Do you have any memos where these points were discussed?" "Did you by chance keep any notes on the meetings?" "Would you mind if I looked through your files on the program?"

In addition, talk to people who are in the business of reviewing and storing program-related materials. A local academician should be up to date on recent publications and might point you to some important documents. A local librarian could help you with various indexes to books and periodicals, or direct you to a bibliography or a reference work. An agency might have collected all the material published on the program. A secretary might describe the agency record-keeping procedures, point to a "pack rat" with cartons of information stashed away, suggest things to read, or open up files for your inspection. If you don't ask, you may miss a lot of important data.

You also need to do a bit of directed exploring. Jot down the titles of books in the offices of key officials and review them later. Take time to browse the shelves of the agency library. Pick up everything available from the publications office. Skim pamphlets and reports on coffee tables or in display cases. While waiting for an appointment, there's hardly ever a time that you should not be reading a document, observing your surroundings, or getting advice on other documents from a helpful secretary.

Finally, you need to follow up the leads provided by the documents themselves: citations to other reports, quotations from a memo, or a table from a book. An analyst describes the process:

> I didn't rely just on people's words. I read everything that was ever published. . . . The biggest problem I had initially was to find out what kind of information was available. I would call the people . . . [in the unit] and say, "Here's the kind of information I want to get. Do you have it?" . . . And in reading one set of documents I would discover that there was this advisory committee that had minutes and I would say, "I want to see all the minutes," and the one girl said, "They are all in that drawer." I said, "May I use your office?" And she said, "Yes." And I just sat at her desk and went through the whole thing and read everything in it.[14]

In short, like every method, document analysis has its problems, but it is an important tool in conducting a first-rate evaluation of a government program.

6

Analyzing and Writing

ANALYSIS IS AN ongoing process, occurring in each stage of program evaluation, as touched on in the preceding chapters. But it also involves gradually pulling everything together and making sense of the program being evaluated, and presenting your findings and recommendations in a convincing way. This information will go in your final report, which generally should include background (program origins, legislative history, goals, early days); a description and analysis of the program's operation; material on goal-related results; conclusions and recommendations; and a section on methodology.

Analysis entails drawing inferences about what the data show, mean, explain, and imply. It requires decisions about what data to exclude, what to emphasize, and how to group and order them. Analysis and writing are inextricably entwined. The very process of putting your ideas on paper leads to new twists, novel arguments, and better ways of understanding the material. At bottom, analysis is thinking and writing clearly.

At a practical level, the role of the analyst is much like that of detective and prosecuting attorney rolled into one, although the analyst typically starts with more clues than a detective and is less of an advocate than a prosecutor. Wiseman notes:

Starting with a few clues, the detective questions persons connected with the case, develops hunches, questions further on the basis of these hunches, begins to see a picture of "what happened" start to emerge, looks for evidence pro and con, elaborating or modifying that picture—until finally the unknown is known. The murderer is caught; what was once a mystery is now understandable. The facts have been "organized" in a way to accommodate—with as few contradictions as possible—the largest amount of empirical data.[1]

But it is not enough for the case to be solved in the analyst's mind. He must convince a jury of skeptical readers. Here enters the prosecuting attorney, as described by Trimble:

Even before the trial actually gets under way, our prosecutor is already about his important first business, which is sizing up the nature of his audience, the rather motley jury (analogous to your *readers*). . . .

. . . the prosecutor spends the bulk of his remaining time calling forth witnesses (the *evidence*) to prove his case. . . .All the while, though, he is doing a number of equally important other things: foxily anticipating and defusing the contentions of the defendant's lawyer; demonstrating his own mastery of the facts of the case; clarifying what's really at issue and what's not; defining his exotic legal terms so that the jury can make sense of them; supporting each new assertion with a wealth of factual proof; quoting authorities . . .; underscoring the logical sequence of his evidence; . . . Finally he makes a closing appeal to the jurors (the *conclusion*) in which he neatly recapitulates the high points of his case. . . .[2] (Emphasis in original.)

Even as your role as an analyst is the combined one of detective and prosecutor, your role in the field is a dual one: while collecting information, you simultaneously analyze it. You make decisions about what data are important and valid, and what hunches hold water. You categorize points, identify themes, think about structure, and develop your conclusions. All of this is tentative, but ideally you are deep into the analysis before you finally start to write up your findings.

In the following discussion, the process of analyzing and writing is split into four sections. The first two sections examine work started in the field: checking out hunches, and various other analytic activities. The last two sections examine office-based writing procedures, and various activities that might help you out if you become stuck in your thinking or writing.

Despite these suggestions, much of the process of analysis remains invulnerable to codification. The intricacies of how the mind processes fieldwork data are not well understood and vary from individual to individual. And it is easier to list some of the components of analysis than to say how to do it. Consequently, this chapter is offered with sympathy toward the view, to paraphrase a scholar, that the fieldworker "has no other method than to do his damndest."[3]

I. CHECKING OUT HUNCHES

You start an evaluation with a set of questions and issues, and hunches about what you will find. A major analytic activity that begins in the field is checking out the plausibility of these hunches—these hypotheses and tentative conclusions brought to the field as well as developed while collecting data. Some hunches involve the *characteristics* of a single program ("The science project primarily serves gifted children"). Others involve the *frequency* with which characteristics exist in a population ("Most of the teachers support the project"). Still others involve *causation* ("The focus on gifted children results from political pressure"). Different types of hunches require different procedures for checking them out. Because of their importance, appropriate procedures are discussed here in detail, in ascending order of complexity.[4]

Hunches About Characteristics

Some hunches involve purported statements of fact: "Codified procedures exist for the selection of children." "The project has been monitored monthly by the state." The procedures for checking out these factual statements were covered in the Chapter 3 discussion of data quality control. Other hunches about characteristics, however, involve the drawing of inferences: "The program director is quite effective." "The project is corrupt." "The decision process was marked by acrimonious bargaining." Here you need to decide what evidence would confirm or disconfirm the hunch, then set out to collect data of both kinds.

Take for example the hunch, "The project is corrupt." Confirming evidence would be valid data showing a pattern of payoffs; disconfirming evidence would be data showing that the staff was hired on a merit basis. As the data were collected from a variety of sources, you would match them with the hunch. If inconsistencies developed, the hunch might be rejected or modified. If the data were essentially consistent with the hunch, you would begin to believe in its credibility; the more the data match the hunch, the more credible it becomes.

In short, checking out hunches about the characteristics of a single entity is relatively straightforward. It is here that fieldwork methods excel.

Hunches About Frequencies

Analysts, however, often want to go further, to demonstrate the plausibility of hunches involving the distribution of characteristics among a particular population: "Inefficiency is *widespread* among program directors." "The *majority* of welfare workers don't understand the regulations." "Projects are *typically* marked by corruption." "*Most* administrators oppose the program." Each of these hunches makes a statement about the frequency of cases.

Checking out such hunches requires the procedures discussed above, but in an *adequate sample* of the population. The conventional approach to sampling is to develop a statistically sound, random sample as described in texts on statistics. As a practical matter, however, you will usually have neither the time nor the resources to pick such a sample and then collect the necessary data. And if the need for a sample arises while you are collecting data at a particular site, you probably won't have much chance to develop a random sample on the spot. Or the population may be so small that random sampling doesn't make sense. However, there are feasible alternatives for developing frequency statements, which should be as precise as possible to sustain the accuracy and credibility of your report.

One alternative is to collect data only from crucial members of the population, following the procedures described in Chapter 2 for selecting crucial sites. Suppose, for example, that you had a hunch that most teachers in the school were opposed to a project. You might interview several teachers generally expected to support the project. If even they were opposed, this would lend some credibility to your original hunch.

Another alternative is to collect data from most of the population. Suppose that the hunch, "The majority of welfare workers don't understand the regulations," is being explored in a welfare office with twelve workers. Time might permit the collection of data from, say, nine workers; if seven fit the hunch, it would be on solid ground. If there were sixty workers it would be impossible to use this approach, but you could say, "Of nine welfare workers contacted, of a total of sixty, seven did not understand the regulations.⁴

Another alternative is to use words such as "several" and "many," when it is difficult to characterize your sample or you are not sure of the total population. These words let you use the information available without overstating your findings.

A final alternative is to quote someone familiar with the program: "According to a respected observer, most project directors . . .'' or ''The principal said that teacher understanding is widespread. . . .'' Although such quotes are not as credible as firsthand data, they are useful when you can't collect the data yourself and your sources are reliable.

Hunches About Causation[5]

Policymakers always want to know whether the government program being evaluated has made a difference. Consequently, the evaluation will inevitably contain statements that causally link funding legislation with changes in procedures or results. Examples of such propositions include: ''The number of patients served has increased because of the new state program.'' ''The improved services result from the new state money.'' ''The legislation explains the new interest in welfare recipients.''

To fully test causal statements linking two variables, experimental design and statistical analysis are required. Nonetheless, fieldwork methods can lead to useful, tentative conclusions, by carefully exploring two basic questions.

The first question is: Did the purported changes actually take place after the law's enactment? This question presents no problem at all in many cases, particularly with legislation establishing something new. You can easily identify a new building, for example, or a new project added to a governmental bureaucracy. But with legislation designed to expand existing activities, the purported changes are not so obvious, and may in fact predate the legislation. For example, a recent law might seem responsible for a strong training program for the unemployed. But later you might discover that it was strong prior to the law and hasn't changed since.

Here you want to examine whether anything actually took place by comparing conditions before and after the program's introduction. Ideally, this involves measuring key variables prior to the program's advent, then measuring them again after the program has been in operation. Typically, though, the ''before'' data were never collected, so you must gather retrospective evidence about what things were like before the program. Collecting valid information about the past, as noted previously, is much harder than collecting it about the present, but it is possible. By comparing past data with current data, you can isolate those things that cannot be attributed to the law because they were in evidence prior to the law's enactment.

Once it has been established that something happened after the program was instituted, the second question is: Did it happen *because* of the legislation? Here you must systematically explore potential rival explanations. For example, a recent state law might seem responsible for an increase in parent participation in the schools. But later you might discover that it resulted from a federal mandate, or from a newly active parent organization, or from all three.

The most common rival explanations involve events apart from the program being evaluated. For example, if a school's administration has substantially improved, it could mean that a state program has been effective, or it could mean that the local board of education replaced the old principal, or it could mean both. If postprogram tutoring services exceed preprogram services, it could mean that a federally supported tutoring program worked, or it might reflect independent volunteer help from parents.

A second set of rival explanations involves changes in program participants as a result of the passage of time. For example, if juvenile delinquents become responsible citizens after a five-year program, it could mean that the program worked or it could mean that the teenagers had simply matured over time. If students perform less well after three hours of instruction, it might mean that their lesson was counterproductive, or it might simply mean that they were tired.

A final rival explanation involves changes in the instrument— the analyst—over time. For example, an improvement in the welfare program's administration during a six-month period might reflect a genuine change or it might reflect a more sympathetic observer.

Other causal relationships that concern the fieldworker involve variables within the program itself: "The program started late because of difficulty in hiring staff"; "The project director's inaction can be attributed to fear of political retribution"; "The management problem resulted from confusion over state regulations"; "The project director quit out of frustration"; "The allocation of funds can be explained by political bargaining." In all of these examples, the focus is on identifying those factors that explain a single event or piece of behavior.

In checking out hunches such as these, you should proceed along the same lines as above. Attention is paid to the sequence of events and to potential rival explanations; you are concerned with when, how, and why something happened. Suppose, for example, that you wanted to check out the hunch, "The program started late because of difficulty in hiring staff." Through document analysis and interviewing, you would collect retrospective data on the sequence of events leading up to the program's late start. You might ask program administrators, "What were things like before the program?" "Why did it start late?" You would explore a variety of rival explanations for the late start, such as a dispute over who should run the program, slowness in getting bureaucratic clearances, political opposition, or lack of agency interest.

You might also systematically compare your sample of sites. Look for a second site where the program did *not* start late, and see how the two sites differ in important ways. If the second site, too, had difficulty in hiring staff, explore other reasons for the first site's late start. You might discover that only the late-starting site has a weak chief administrator. If this is corroborated in other sites (a tardy program with a weak administrator, a timely program with a strong administrator), all the better. You have another possible explanation. Typically, you will find a variety of explanatory factors.[6]

In cases like this, where the event being explained and the explanation are separated by only a few intervening variables (as contrasted with, say, linking the impact of a government program to the reduction of poverty), you are in a relatively good position to discover plausible explanations. But even here, given the difficulty in eliminating rival explanations, the wise analyst is reluctant to draw ironclad conclusions.

In sum, you should try to determine when something happened, be alert to rival explanations and explore them, and recognize the tentativeness of cause-effect findings; humility should be the guiding virtue. However, tentative findings can be better than none at all, and even if they are not definitive, they do suggest further questions which can help in the effort to determine whether a government program is really working.

II. OTHER ANALYTIC ACTIVITIES

As you check out your hunches, you are also involved in a variety of other analytic activities, alert to any information that will help put the program in perspective, while you develop the central ideas of your assessment. This is helped by getting feedback from your colleagues and others as discussed in Chapter 3. Several other related activities are highlighted here.

Exploring

In addition to examining the issues brought to the field, be on the lookout also for other important data. This might be information illustrating a current issue (for example, if the legislature is concerned about government spending, an example of efficiency). It might be data providing a novel way to look at a problem (for example, how students view procedural safeguards controlling school suspensions). It might be data on the concerns of program administrators (for example, the legislature's late appropriation of program money), or it might be information showing a deviation from accepted practice, common expectations, shared goals or prevailing assumptions (for example, data showing that court delays are not caused by case backlogs). Deviations should trigger a search for explanations.

Whatever the category, you are constantly sifting the data for program-related material that may be important to your audiences. This sifting process consists mainly of questioning the data: Is this information important? Why? What does it illustrate? What does it mean? Where does it lead?

Categorizing

A unique human trait is the ability to categorize, to put things in boxes like a postal worker sorting mail. It brings order to data and is necessary for examining relationships. It is essential to human existence, yet often taken for granted. If, for example, newspaper ads were not divided and subdivided into various categories, just imagine trying to compare the properties of various Volkswagens or to draw relationships between makes of cars and prices.

In program evaluation, categorizing must start in the early days of data collection and continue until the final report. All the while, you are refining preliminary categories, deleting some and adding others, spelling out the attributes of each classification and sub-classification, and drawing relationships among them.

Some categories depend on your conceptual framework, or assumptions about what data are important; a conceptual code helps you sort the data. For example, you might begin by grouping the data into the categories discussed in Chapter 1— "organizational and political setting," "essential program features," "key individuals and institutions," etc. Under program features, you might subdivide the data into key facts: *What* are the issues and problems? *When* did they occur? *How* did they develop? *Where* did they exist? *Who* was involved? *Why* did they develop?

Other categories depend on the content of the program area being studied. In education, for example, school staff can be divided into teachers, administrators, and ancillary staff. Administrators can be further divided into superintendents, business officers, and principals.

Still other categories will emerge from your immersion in the data. For example, in writing Chapter 3, I made a long list of sources of bias and error, and then sorted them into three categories—"the analyst," "the subject," and "the situation." Under "the subject," I subclassified the problems into subject ability and cooperation. Of course, the list of things that can be classified, and the way they can be grouped, is endless.[7]

To cope with your ever-increasing categories, it is virtually essential to develop a filing system. You might start with separate files that correspond to the general topics you expect to cover in the final report—program characteristics, methodology, recommendations, etc. You might also keep a separate set of folders for each site visited. As the study progresses and narrower categories develop, establish corresponding folders. These files can hold documents collected in the field, interview notes, jottings about ways to organize or interpret the data, and cross-references to other material.

Some fieldworkers go beyond a filing system and develop a detailed coding scheme for sorting data into hundreds or thousands of categories and subcategories. They then cut up their field notes and place the scraps of paper in corresponding folders or attach them to index cards. Such detailed coding makes sense in long-term studies involving thousands of pages of notes. But in a several-month study, the type this book describes, detailed coding may not be necessary if you cross-reference and remember the details of your filing system.[8]

Distilling Themes

In program evaluation, as in music, one looks for themes, those principal ideas that recur throughout the data. A major theme in a study of handicapped children might be the complexity of adequately serving the multiple-handicapped. A major theme in the Connecticut compensatory education evaluation was the widespread confusion about which children to serve. Identified themes can lead to the exploration of previously unidentified relationships, perhaps the discovery of further themes. The major themes can be stressed in the final report, and might be used as an organizing device for presenting the data.

Generating New Slants

Out of this process of examining hunches, exploring new data, and categorizing and distilling themes, might come a markedly different view of the program. The focus of the study might change entirely. For example, if you are looking for goal-related results, but discover that the program is not yet in place, switch the focus to implementation. You might develop new categories and identify additional themes that were not obvious from the start. You might generate new hypotheses, often more complex than the original ones. These hunches might reflect discussions with colleagues, outside reading, observed repetitions in the data, or observed relationships among the preliminary classifications. Hunches generated in the field can often lead to the most significant findings.

Developing Your Theses

The final document will present a few major theses (arguments) about the character of the program, its problems and the reasons for them, and some recommended changes. Your statements will be arguments in that you will try to use your accumulated evidence to persuade the reader that your inferences, interpretations, and suggestions follow from the data. For example, suppose you found that social workers in a particular town worked nights and weekends. Instead of listing this work pattern in a section describing the local program, it might be used as an illustration in a section arguing that the program is understaffed.

The deeper you get into the study, the more you try to hone your overall arguments. Hunches are checked out, modified, or rejected. Think less of new ideas, and more of what the data mean, what they imply, and where they lead. All this is tentative, but major arguments, conclusions, and recommendations are beginning to take shape.

Developing an Overall Structure

While you are in the field, you need to begin thinking about a master plan for presenting your data and conclusions. This involves the overall organization of the document—the major chapters and sections and their sequence. It requires logically grouping and ordering the data in a way that highlights your key points.

There are a number of ways to arrange your material. Because every program has a beginning, a middle, and an end (cutoff point), a common approach is to present your data in chronological order. Alternatively, the data might be grouped by themes or topics. For example, a study of handicapped children might be arranged according to different handicapping conditions. Still another approach is case studies where the story of the program is told separately for each of the sites visited.

In any given evaluation, you might have a combination of these or other arrangements for organizing your material. For example, a report might be divided into case studies that present each story chronologically through paragraphs arranged in a general-to-specific order. Because devising a logical structure is one of your hardest and most important tasks, it is essential to begin thinking about it early.[9]

Recording Analytic Thoughts

While in the field, there is a mechanical procedure that helps considerably in analyzing the data—the preparation of what might be called analytic memos. Such memos provide an opportunity to periodically take stock of what is going on and what has been learned. They can record flashes of insight, emerging themes, new categories, books or articles to be read, or points to look up. The overall purpose is to start the process of making sense out of the data, to summarize what you know, and to provide a guide for what to do next.

III. WRITING IT UP

At some point, finally, you leave the field to seek solitude and write up your report. You might leave because you are "ready to write"; you know you can describe key program characteristics and present your conclusions and recommendations. Or you might have reached a saturation level; you're hearing the same points over and over again. More often than not, however, you will leave the field because you must if you have any hope of meeting your deadline, and writing usually takes much longer than novices expect. In any case, the time comes to withdraw and try to make sense on paper of all the data, interpretations, and puzzles spinning in your head.[10]

This can be a painful experience, as a novice evaluator found out:

> Without the deadline, we wouldn't have written. We would have continued to postpone the day of reckoning at our typewriters and compulsively pursued the details of our argument. . . . For me, writing was painful—not because I was struggling with the fine points of diction and phrasing, but because I had to disengage from the intrigue of detective work and concentrate on making sense of so much information. It had been exhilarating to pursue a hunch—one clue led

> to another. But writing was burdensome. It was hard to lift
> everything out of storage and rearrange it in a new structure
> of ideas. The mental move exhausted me.[11]

At this stage, different analysts proceed in markedly different ways. Some develop lengthy, detailed outlines, then write good first drafts. Others don't use outlines at all, thinking through the issues in their heads and drafting their reports as they write. Some rigorously produce a few pages a day while others write furiously all at once. Some writers fit their approach to the complexity of the material. Obviously, there is no single best way.

What follows, then, is not "the ideal approach" to writing an evaluation report, but a summary of techniques, gleaned from others and from my experience, that helps me cope with complicated material. Some of these ideas might work for you, and some might not, but they might help you experiment to find the techniques best for you. In describing the process, I rely heavily on examples of how this chapter was put together. Like many analysts, I don't normally think much about the process of writing, I just knuckle down and do it. In preparing this chapter, however, I kept notes as I went along. This chapter was quite difficult for me, so writing about how it was written illustrates how one analyst dealt with complicated material.

Reflecting on Your Notes

During data collection, you accumulate mounds of materials: memos, program descriptions, letters, application forms, newspaper clippings, field notes, notes on your readings and interviews, jottings on important ideas, analytic memos. Before writing, it pays to spend a day or two reviewing all this material. This refreshes your memory of your preliminary data, arguments, themes, and overall structure, and pushes you forward to write a draft.

While rereading, I constantly make notes on my notes. Some

include important points to incorporate in the report ("need to emphasize Tom Jones' role in the program's administration—see interview notes of 1/3"). Some spotlight arguments ("stress that the program was poorly managed—see Audit Report, p. 43"). Others stress structure ("maybe chronological order would make sense"). Still others might note new ideas, things to exclude, books to read, sections to include, questions to pursue, or quotes that should be included somewhere.

Out of this process of reading, thinking, and note-making should emerge enough ideas to develop into a rough outline. Referring to this chapter, I noted:

> What I've done this morning is review my notes and make notes on my notes—groping toward a tentative design or group of categories for organizing the data. I've made the analytic decision to deal with the analytic process in time sequence (could have done differently). Now I want to move toward a rough outline of various sections of the chapter and then group various things to include in the outline. . . . Then, with that in hand, I am prepared to write a very rough draft, I think.

The wheat is being separated from the chaff, and the important strains of wheat are being identified. Through emphasis, elimination, and interpretation, the analyst imposes order on the data.

Making an Initial Outline

An outline translates your emerging ideas into a preliminary overall structure. It splits your project into major sections and lists and organizes your points, providing a concrete guide to writing a draft. Your files can be rearranged to match the headings. At this stage, the outline may be fairly rough and, like your first draft, likely to change.

The first crude outline for this chapter contained two parts and nine sections. Part I consisted of: (1) introduction; (2) what the analyst brings to the field; (3) early stages; (4) later stages; and (5) what the analyst leaves the field with. Part II included: (1) reread notes; (2) develop a rough outline; (3) the first draft; and (4) postfirst draft. Various points to be included were listed under each of these headings. For example, the Introduction section listed:

-- define analysis
-- say what chapter is
-- contrast with quantitative stuff/changing character of analysis
-- put analysis and writing together because they are inextricably intertwined
-- need to talk about the process being highly individualistic—also depends on the problem and scope of the research. Here are some things that work for some people.

After listing the points I wanted to make in each section, I put the remaining points, which did not fit those sections, in a miscellaneous category at the end of the outline to be dealt with or discarded later.

The next step is to refine the outline or move on to a draft. I find the latter course useful—dealing with one major section or chapter at a time—when I'm not sure of what to say, because it propels me onward.

Writing a First Draft

If the material is fairly straightforward or if you are under the gun to finish the report, write the first draft directly for your intended audience. With a bit of editing and polishing, the result will be adequate.

But if the material is puzzling and you have time to write more than one main draft, you might write the first one for yourself— a private draft—instead of for your audience. A private draft entails writing madly, taking the notes in your rough outline and putting them into prose, not worrying about just the right words, syntax, transitions, grouping, or sequence. The idea is to get out on paper all the facts, arguments, inferences, and ideas buzzing around in your head. Keep going even when you encounter holes in your arguments, missing data, or leaps of logic. My first private draft for this chapter was twenty-two handwritten pages written in about five hours.

Writing a private draft can serve several useful purposes. First, it can be a memory device. Before your thoughts are spelled out on paper, a lot of energy can go into remembering what you want to say and how you think you want to say it; a private draft can ease this burden. Second, it can be a liberating device. It is often hard to start writing, especially if you think the first draft has to be good and ought to be shared. Writing an expectedly awful private draft takes the pressure off and may enable you to get into the rhythm of writing. It gives you some text to work with, even though that version may end up in the wastebasket.

Most important, a private draft can be a problem-solving device. The very process of getting things down on paper will help identify weak spots and important issues, and help generate new ideas and insights. Ideas beget ideas. Also, without a draft it is often difficult to see how different ideas, floating around in your head, fit together; it is much easier to cut up and shuffle pieces of paper containing written text.

A private draft won't work for people who censor and criticize their ideas in the process of writing, or become locked into the words that come out; if they write a draft too soon, important ideas might be excluded. For these people, it's probably best to concentrate on a detailed outline before writing text. For others, it is enough to consciously suspend judgment, to remember that the purpose of a private draft is to spill out all your ideas in words that can easily be changed, and not to criticize your thoughts or allow others to.

Recycling

Progressing from a first draft of complicated material to a finished product normally involves a series of "re's." You reread your notes, reoutline your material, rewrite the section, rethink your arguments, relocate your points, rearrange your presentation, remove irrelevancies, and refine your prose. You may also return to the field to fill the gaping holes in your data revealed by this recycling. If you start with a private draft, your writing will shift from prose intended to help you think, to prose written with your audience in mind.

Three weeks after writing the first draft of this chapter, and having the time to return to it, I started recycling:

> Today was something of a bummer. I felt like an old car being started, again, in below-freezing weather. It has taken me practically all day to get back into it. Not a very productive day.
>
> What I did:
>
> Reread first draft several times—but generally got stuck on how to proceed. Got hung up on where to discuss the procedures for dealing with correlations, causes, and different kinds of propositions. Tentatively decided to put that stuff in chapter on bias and error. After that decision, I decided to go back over earlier notes plus go back to some of my data. . . .Right now, I'm not ready to write, but I'm more into the stuff than this morning.

As my notes suggest, recycling can also involve reentry problems if you can't stay on the task.

Another step in recycling is reducing your attention to a smaller, manageable segment (for example, a section of a chapter) and repeating the steps followed at the broader level. The other sections, and files associated with them, are put aside (and out of mind) until you have a decent new draft for this segment. My notes two weeks later:

> The last few days I've been working on draft #2 of the chapter. . . . [After making cross-references in the margins,] I picked out some sections of the chapter that were particularly troublesome and decided to concentrate on these manageable chunks. . . . For each of these sections, I made a rough outline. . .listing the points to be included with some attention to sequence (although I'm still not sure where the sections fit overall). . . . Next I wrote drafts of the sections. One yesterday, another today. . . . Overall I'm trying to strengthen troubling sections by narrowing the breadth of what I attack in one sitting, but expanding the depth. By concentrating on troubling parts early on, I can be thinking about them as I work on other things.

Section by section, you hone the argument, strengthen the grouping, improve the sequence, and (often painfully) excise material that doesn't fit.

When I'm reasonably comfortable with the various sections, it's time to return to the bigger picture and put them together into the chapter, working on sequence, grouping, and transitions. My notes a few days later:

> It's 11:35 a.m. and I'm really tired. I seem to have already run out of steam. I want to finish another draft of the analysis chapter today, but I don't see how I am going to manage to do so. . . .
>
> Surprise, surprise. After a long (30-minute) lunch break, I came back fresh and ready to go. My motivation was also enhanced by a call . . . urging me to finish. Armed with new spirit and the prod, I worked over part of the beginning of the

chapter and inserted the pieces that I had done during the
week. I now have a new draft of the chapter on analysis . . .
Now, since I have to return to other things, I will let the stuff
marinate.

This process continues until the individual pieces of a chapter are
clear and well argued, and fit together into a coherent whole.

As the different chapters take shape, you can compare them for
content and style, and with scissors and stapler in hand move
pieces around. A conclusion may become an introduction, a dan-
gling section may be dropped because it doesn't fit into the argument, or a segment of one chapter may belong in a different
chapter. Once the pieces are properly arranged, you can work on
your transitions and do some final editing. You are close to being
done.

Letting Go

Recycling and refining, in the absence of deadlines, could go on
forever. There is always room to develop new ideas, explore new
twists, hone your arguments, and sharpen your presentation. Indeed, Truman Capote claims that he never finishes a book; his
publishers come and take it away.[12]

So, too, in program evaluation, a time comes to let go even
though the report is incomplete or imperfect. A time comes to
move on to something else. You'll get this message from your
friends, family, and bosses. You'll also get it from yourself. Take
the message, meet your deadlines, and let go.

IV. Getting Unstuck

No matter how well our techniques may work, we all get "stuck"
from time to time. Faced with a pile of information, you don't
know quite what to make of it. You don't know what is important

and why, what it proves (if anything), or how to turn the chaos into intelligent prose. You know you have a serious block but you can't even articulate its specific character. You just can't write.

Faced with this, many novices begin to believe that their misery, loss for words, and confusion is clear evidence that they cannot write or think, and thus they dwell on their perceived incompetence rather than the task. Others go to extraordinary lengths to avoid grappling with their blockages. I know one analyst who, quite out of character, started giving Tupperware parties to avoid biting the analytic bullet. I know another who badly burned her writing arm and upon reflection, thought she might have acted unconsciously, making it impossible to work.

Thinking and writing are hard work even for the most gifted. Hemingway, for instance, rewrote his material constantly, writing thirty-nine drafts of the last part of *A Farewell to Arms*.[13] Thinking and writing require concentration, persistence, endurance, discipline, and commitment. Many professionals, in the act of writing, are obsessed by their work, oblivious to others, moody about their progress, and troubled by self-doubt. Edgar Allan Poe's comments on fiction apply equally well to the nonfiction of program evaluation:

> Most writers prefer having it understood that they compose by a species of fine frenzy—an ecstatic intuition, and would positively shudder at letting the public take a peep behind the scenes, at the elaborate and vascillating crudities of thought—at the true purposes seized only at the last moment—at the fully-matured fancies discarded in despair as unmanageable—at the cautious selections and rejections—at the painful erasures and interpolations—in a word, at the wheels and pinions—the stepladders and demon traps, the cock's feathers, the red paint and black patches, which in ninety-nine cases out of the hundred, constitute the properties of the literary histrio.[14]

But it is not enough to know that you are in good company. What specifically can *you* do to get unstuck, or to avoid getting stuck?

You need to diagnose your problems and experiment with various ways to make progress. While there's no sure prescription, here are ten concrete suggestions. In practice, they often overlap and can be used in combination. For the novice, the key is to recognize that blockages are a normal part of the process, and they can be successfully overcome by trying different approaches until something works.

Creating a Writer's Nest

A common problem is that the novice tries to write in an environment filled with distractions—noises, people, telephones, irrelevant books to read. He also might try to adopt a style of work in conflict with his basic temperament. You're expected to work during the day at your office desk. Experienced writers create a supportive environment and indulge their eccentricities. Kant wrote in bed with his blankets especially arranged. Schiller filled his desk with rotten apples. Frost wrote on a writing board, often on the sole of his shoe. Hemingway stood on the worn skin of an antelope when he wrote, in a pair of oversized loafers.[15] I write at a table in a renovated chicken coop without a phone.

To write a program evaluation it may not be necessary to go to such extremes, but it is important to develop a supportive environment that matches your needs and that is free from outside distractions. You might find a quiet, vacant office or a corner of a library, or establish a workplace in a room of your own. It also pays to get in the habit of working in that spot each day—morning, noon, or night, whatever works—for a set period of time.

Examining the Risks

Another common problem, often not acknowledged, is that the writer is scared to death. Unlike conversation, where you can clarify thoughts in response to cues and questions, written views

[153]

hang out there, permanently, to be picked apart by people you do not even know. It seems easy to make a fool of yourself, or to be misunderstood. Writing is thus perceived as a high-risk venture.

Realistically, however, the risks are probably nowhere near as high as they seem. For one thing, just because you have spent every waking hour on your prose and know its every weakness, this doesn't mean that the reader will notice; in most cases, his involvement is much less intense than yours. Readers who do notice are probably more forgiving than many novices think. If your report shows an earnest effort to cope with the material and a sincere concern for the reader's need for clear prose, weaknesses, even small errors, will be discounted.

Thinking Small

Agonizing over "everything I've got to do to finish" can block you completely, panic and procrastination growing with each passing hour and day. If this is a problem, remember that you can progress steadily by working at any given time on just a tiny segment of the report. Establish a deadline, make a reasonable schedule, work at it every day, and take each manageable chunk of material a step at a time. For example, a seventy-page report due in two weeks can be conceived of as five good pages a day. Writing in "takes" this way can help enormously, as one novice reflected after her first evaluation:

> . . . I will be undyingly grateful for . . . [the] tip on writing "takes" instead of feeling that the whole story must be told in one sweep. That's the surest way I have found to circumvent blocks, and to get going with what you have. My tendency is to try and frame the whole thing either in my mind or on scraps of paper. Sometimes that process just doesn't do the trick. Writing in segments and then seeing how the segments fit together has already proven itself as a viable method for me.[16]

Rethinking Your Assumptions

Many writing problems are not writing problems at all; they are thinking problems. Even skilled writers cannot translate fuzzy thinking into clear prose. One good way to handle such problems is to rethink your assumptions.

A basic assumption is like the first turn on a trip. If you take the wrong one, you will be lost until you discover your mistake. In doing an analysis, it is common to make a series of assumptions (both conscious and unconscious), promptly forget that they were made, then fail to check them when the analysis goes nowhere. It pays to return to square one, and ask: What assumptions am I making? What would happen if I substituted different assumptions?

You might explore different concepts that provide a new perspective on the data. Something previously overlooked or ignored might pull together some of the unsorted data. Reconsider your assumptions about what data to include in the report. Data excluded earlier might be important now. You might challenge your assumptions about how the report should be organized. If you've assumed that a case study format would work, but the data don't fit, try another format and see if things fit better.

Working Backwards

Since the Golden Age of Greece, mathematicians have counseled their students to work backwards in solving complicated problems. Starting with what is to be proved, you ask what step is required to reach this proof, what step is required to reach the next-to-last step, what is required to reach the step before that, and so on until you have worked your way back to known information. This reverse process is typically hidden from view, because the solution is presented as if you proceeded directly.[17]

In conducting an evaluation, you may end up wallowing around in a pile of unorganized data and arguments. Try working backwards, systematically addressing a series of questions, and you might discover what's missing in your effort to provide a logical analysis. Just what are you trying to prove? (for example, "The local project is poorly managed.") To reach this conclusion, what kinds of data would you need? (An audit report, quotes from state officials, observations of chaotic procedures.) Have you collected these data? (You have the audit report and observations, but no quotes.) How could the missing data be collected? (You need to interview the state director and the local program coordinator.)

Adjusting Your Lens

Imagine a photographer with a zoom lens on his camera taking a picture across a large meadow from a friend's back porch. He can capture the full landscape, a rolling hill, a stand of pines, a lone flower, or a blade of grass. The results depend upon how he adjusts his lens.

The same is true for program analysts. Sometimes we get lost in details, unable to see the forest for the trees. Other times, the problem is the reverse and we get lost in the overall organization of the report. In both cases, just as the photographer moves back and forth from the whole to a small detail, the evaluator must try to adjust his lens. If you are getting nowhere in trying to figure out the big picture, try working out some of the details. If you are having difficulty with details, try to focus on the larger issues. Changing the focus can keep the analysis going because you shift gears to something new. It can also lead to new combinations of data, with a focus on details helping you see the bigger picture, and vice versa.

Shuffling and Comparing

In addition to shifting the way you look at the data, it might also help to shift the data themselves, comparing different pieces in different configurations. One possibility is to arrange your data into sequential patterns so you can compare changes across time. For example, you might examine the evolution of the state's monitoring procedures, comparing their consequences at different points in the program's history. Another possibility is to arrange your data according to their organizational origins. For example, you could examine state monitoring across various sites, comparing the different responses. A third possibility is to rearrange the data so they can be compared with something familiar that is analogous to the problem. Analogies suggest questions for you to ask about the data, and in the final report they can help the reader make sense out of complicated material. This shuffling and comparing regularly involves scissors and stapler as drafts are cut up and rearranged.

Attacking the Flank

Sometimes it makes sense to approach an analytic problem indirectly. The questions become: Am I familiar with a related issue? An analogous issue? A more general case of the issue? A more special case of the issue? How can I learn about related problems? One indirect approach is to draw on experience for examples of related material. Another approach is to read material only slightly related to what you are working on. While thinking about writing this section, I turned to books on the creative process and on solving mathematical problems.[18]

If you were concerned about managerial behavior in an education agency, you might read about a policy problem in a health agency, an article on welfare management, or a magazine piece about governmental reorganization. Slightly related material often suggests new categories for organizing data, persuasive arguments, or novel ways of thinking about an issue.

Sleeping on It

Sometimes you attack a problem from every conceivable angle, but still remain stuck. If this happens, walk away from the problem completely and do something else—sleep, exercise, play—and get your mind off the problem. After a break, relaxed and ready for a fresh start, you often can return to the puzzle, achieve a sudden breakthrough, and be immediately certain about the solution.

A variant of this dilemma is the plateau; you know you could do better, but progress has leveled off. Here it might pay to put these issues in the back of your mind and concentrate on something else. The hope is that different issues will blend and work together over time. Indeed, it is because of the time it takes to solve complicated problems that it pays to start working early on troublesome issues. Analytical solutions, like venison, profit from marination.

Pestering Other People

Sometimes the best way to get unstuck is to seek help from individuals with different, fresh perspectives. Colleagues might be able to diagnose the problem with ease. A major issue may be buried in the text, characteristics and causes may be mixed up, the organization scheme may be getting in the way of thinking, or an important interpretation may be overlooked. Seek help even if you are unable to clearly define the problem. If several colleagues with different perspectives can be consulted, all the better.

In addition, when your friends and relatives ask how you are doing, lunge at the opportunity and seek their advice. Talking in nontechnical terms with people unfamiliar with the issues can often lead to helpful suggestions. Many of the ideas presented here were developed over dinner or through chance discussions with neighbors, relatives, and friends.

7

Summing Up
and Applying Standards

AFTER ALL IS said and done, the value of an evaluation report hinges on well-supported conclusions and well-thought-out recommendations. The preceding chapter focused on the *process* of completing the report—analyzing the data and writing them up. This chapter focuses on the *substance* of conclusions and recommendations. In addition, I take a look at the overall issue of quality, suggesting standards to apply in putting together a good report after months of investigation, even in the face of a tight deadline.

I. THE CONCLUSIONS

You want your readers to clearly grasp the most important things learned from conducting the evaluation. This requires careful presentation of straightforward descriptive facts, as illustrated in the Chapter 1 discussion of program operations. It also means going beyond the mosaic of data to present conclusions that say what something logically means, what it implies, what it signifies, what it is worth, and what it suggests as next steps. Conclusions can be drawn about the characteristics, causes, implementation, impact, and improvement of a program, as well as the goals themselves. Conclusions can be general or specific, tentative or certain, weak or strong. They can be set forth at the end of the report (or at the end of a section), or they can be integrated into the text. Several examples from recent evaluations help demonstrate the variety.

The first example comes from an evaluation of student financial aid in Connecticut:

> The State programs of student financial assistance are *unnecessarily fragmented* into too many individual programs.
> The fragmentation *complicates* administration at the institutional level. . . .[1] (Emphasis added)

This brief excerpt contains conclusions about program characteristics (they are fragmented), about the quality of implementation (*unnecessarily* fragmented), and about the impact of this fragmentation (it complicates administration). To reach these conclusions the analysts needed concrete evidence to document the fragmentation and complication. They also needed a standard of comparison for judging what was "unnecessary."

A second example is excerpted from an evaluation of school accountability in Florida:

> This discussion leads to the following conclusions: First, no one appears to use the data generated by the statewide assessment program. . . . The program's shifting purpose, based upon personnel changes and unclear intent, has caused significant misunderstandings of what the program is capable of doing.[2]

This excerpt contains conclusions about a program characteristic (shifting purpose), about causes (the shifting purposes are attributed to personnel changes and unclear intent), and about program impact (the data were not used, and the shifting purpose led to misunderstandings). To reach these conclusions, the analysts not only needed to assemble supporting evidence, but they also had to check out rival explanations for the shifting purposes and misunderstandings.

Another example comes from a Connecticut compensatory education evaluation:

> Despite the years of experience... and piles of rules and regulations, money is still being expended inappropriately . . . A careful reworking of the program is necessary, and this will require extensive technical assistance from the state.[3]

In this passage, the analysts draw a general conclusion about the appropriate next step (program reworking) and what it will take (technical assistance). They also reach a negative conclusion about the success of implementation (the money is being inappropriately spent). A strong conclusion like this requires a clear standard for judging appropriate expenditure and specific evidence demonstrating that the standard is not being met.

In addition to these types of conclusions, which are chiefly logical deductions from the data, other conclusions interpret the information collected, suggest its meaning and importance, and respond to the question, "so what?" Such an interpretation is sometimes intertwined with description, as illustrated in the Connecticut compensatory education evaluation:

> *Swift passage came because of the formula for distributing resources. . . . This formula, devised prior to the bill's introduction, had the political virtue of not ignoring rural and suburban areas even as it put most of the money in Connecticut cities.* As Senator Gloria Schaeffer pointed out in 1965: "By setting the income level at $4000 or less, we are very conscious and hopeful of the fact that these monies will go not only to large urban communities, but also to the middle size and even to the small towns, where there are families existing at that level."

Since 1965, all of Connecticut's 169 towns have been eligible
for funds. In 1974, 165 towns participated in the program.[4]
(Emphasis added)

In this passage, the italicized section interprets the evidence by
presenting an argument about the significance of the formula (its
political importance). The quotation from Senator Schaeffer and
the figures showing widespread participation provide evidence to
buttress the argument.

Other times, conclusions that interpret the meaning of data stand
by themselves in the narrative. They start with sentences such as:
"This suggests . . .," "The moral of the story is . . .," "The
lessons learned are. . . ." Whether the interpretation is intertwined with the description or stands alone, it should be clear
that *describing* ("The project directors joined forces to lobby on
Capitol Hill") is different from *interpreting* ("For the first time,
the project directors were upset enough to resort to political action;
this may establish a precedent for future encounters"). Because
data typically are open to multiple interpretations, you should be
appropriately cautious in jumping to conclusions.

A special note on conclusions about program goals: If the
evidence suggests that a prevailing standard or expectation is
unrealistic, the final report should say so. If you find that strict
compliance with goals is counterproductive (for example, tight
regulations stifle needed project flexibility), point it out. Similarly,
if a goal is outdated (for example, increasing the supply of
teachers), if a goal appears trivial or inconsequential, or if goals are
fuzzy or conflicting, say so. Alternatively, you might suggest new
goals and standards that more clearly reflect the program's
strengths.

Regardless of the character of the conclusions, drawing them
assumes that you are willing to take the risk of making judgments
and recording them in the report. Your knowledge and insight after
extensive study and thought ought to be tapped to the fullest. But it
should be clear that the more you make judgments, the more you
need to spell out the explicit evidence used and the procedures

followed. The fuzzier the basis for your conclusion, the more detail should be included. The more controversial the conclusion, the more opposing viewpoints should be analyzed. The more you speculate, the more your conclusions should be labeled as such. In all cases, enough detail should be included to allow the reader to reach an independent judgment about what conclusions are appropriate.

II. THE RECOMMENDATIONS

If program evaluation is intended to make things better, it is ironic that recommendations are often treated like the proverbial visiting mother-in-law: Some space is provided, but not much attention. So much time and energy is expended looking at the past that few resources remain to look toward the future. The result is often a recommendations section in an evaluation report that makes few sensible or practical suggestions for improvement.

But program evaluation can generate workable proposals for improvement. You must examine alternatives (recognizing that change is not synonymous with improvement), and present the recommendations in a form that reflects accepted procedures. This requires a familiarity with options that go beyond the common suggestions for better coordination, communication, and reorganization. It also requires considerable effort and a lot of time— almost always more than that allotted.

Time built into the schedule allows you to explore a variety of alternatives and, equally important, to estimate the feasibility of implementing tentative recommendations. For example, it might make little sense (at least in the short run) to recommend abolishing an agency bureau, if it is entrenched and supported by a powerful constituency. Look for less drastic, more feasible suggestions and examine bureaucratic and political obstacles before making recommendations.

But what substantive recommendations are sensible? Knowledge about alternatives might come from prior experience, from reports on similar programs, or from the process of conducting the evaluation. For example, ask program administrators how they think things could be improved; check out with them tentative recommendations. Consumers of the service being provided may have insightful comments about remedies. And you might consult with experts on management or on the substance of the program. For example, if you are evaluating programs for handicapped children, contact someone trained in that field who has a national perspective.

Questionable Recommendations

Whatever the source of the recommendations, be wary of echoing the commonplace, questionable advice of many evaluations—communicate better, coordinate better, and reorganize.

Most, if not all, organizations are thought by some to need improved communication among their staff, and closer coordination among their programs. The usual question is not whether a "problem" exists, but why—and the diagnosis is critical because prescriptions for misdiagnosed problems do not work. The usual diagnosis focuses on the management of the system and the traits of its staff. People do not coordinate or communicate, it is argued, because they are incompetent, psychologically unable, lazy, or poor managers. Therefore, if they learned to be more open, worked harder, or adopted modern management techniques (for example, planning), the problems would be solved.

There is some truth to this analysis, otherwise it probably would not persist in government circles. But there is another diagnosis that focuses less on managerial or staff deficiencies and more on political factors. In this view, different individuals and units have different conceptions of the public good and they recognize the need to compete for scarce public resources. Increased coordination and open communication are viewed as a threat to their power;

this could lead to less resources for their programs and thus for their conception of what society requires. In this analysis, lack of coordination and communication is not the outcome of managerial problems, but a deliberate strategy to maintain control over limited resources. If this political diagnosis is accurate, managerial prescriptions will simply sputter and fade.

Recommendations for reorganization assume that grouping related programs will foster efficiency, reduce duplication, enhance coordination and communication, and ultimately improve government services. Changing the organizational chart is a favorite pastime of governmental reformers.

No doubt benefits can result from reorganization. For one thing, it provides a symbol of change. This can help create momentum and myths about the organization, and these are important in maintaining political support. For another, reorganization can provide a rationale for moving unacceptable staff by reorganizing their jobs out of existence. This makes sense particularly in agencies hemmed in by rigid Civil Service requirements. In addition, reorganization can provide a structure that the reorganizer "owns" and is comfortable defending. And, in some cases, reorganization can in fact help reduce ridiculous inefficiency and mindless duplication, and provide some reasonable coordination.

But one must wonder about the assumptions underlying proposals for reform through reorganization. There is little evidence, for example, that reorganization leads to more efficient, smaller, or cheaper government. There may be fewer boxes on the organizational chart, but rarely are there fewer people or less costly operations. Similarly, there is little evidence that formal changes in organization affect informal ties and lines of communication. Internal and external constituencies often survive structural rearrangement. Furthermore, it is not certain that duplication is bad. Competition for clients just might lead to better government services, as it purportedly does in the private sector.[5]

In addition, many hidden costs are associated with reorganization efforts. First, such efforts inevitably create morale problems because replacing functioning groups with new ones causes frustration that can reduce efficiency. Second, reorganization creates political heat, particularly when a constituency loses its box on the organizational chart. And third, major reorganization inevitably takes much longer to accomplish than anticipated, and consumes the time of the leader in charge. Securing internal clearances, selling the reorganization politically, and dealing with the Civil Service typically become full-time occupations.

All in all, reorganization is overrated as a vehicle for enhancing governmental effectiveness. Its worst vice is that it diverts attention from the tasks the agency should be doing and the problems it should be solving. This is not to say that reorganization or better coordination and communication should never be recommended. But as reform measures they are usually weak, and you would do well to go beyond them in recommending change.

Some Specific Examples

Some examples drawn from recent evaluations illustrate the variety of recommendations possible. Some call for legislative action. This might mean the passage of a bill, public hearings, changes in appropriations, or further investigation.

An evaluation of Connecticut compensatory education recommends:

> ... The legislature should consider requiring the establishment of parent advisory councils in all . . . schools, with the resources and authority to oversee the local implementation of [the program].[6]

A Florida school accountability evaluation advises:

> The Legislature should stipulate, in statute, specific responsibilities of the Department and specific responsibilities of the public school districts for the development and im-

plementation of such an information system, including time-frame for action.[7]

Some recommendations call for administrative action. These recommendations might tighten program compliance procedures or, alternatively, loosen central control helping develop local capacity to implement the program.[8] Specifically, the recommendations might include personnel changes, improved regulations and guidelines, strengthened management procedures, reallocation of manpower and effort, and, under some circumstances, reorganization.

The Connecticut compensatory education evaluation recommends:

> Systematic procedures should be developed for application review, on-site visitations, follow-up activities and reporting on findings.[9]

The Florida accountability evaluation recommends:

> The Department of Education should revise its cost reporting procedures to include federal funds and the funds expended for inservice training.[10]

Some recommendations relate specifically to program costs. A Connecticut financial aid evaluation, for example, undertook an unusually detailed analysis of various ways to administer the state's financial aid program for college students. After examining costs and benefits of various options, the evaluation recommended:

> . . . [establishing] an in-state organization for the administration. . . [of the program]. . . . The establishment of such an organization . . . would entail a first-year cost of approximately $118,000, or $3,000 more than the current cost of the . . . [outside] contracts. In the second year, it is esti-

mated that the cost would be approximately $92,800 or
$22,200 less than the current $115,000 cost. . . .[11]

Some recommendations relate to a timetable for implementing
the primary recommendations. The Connecticut compensatory
education evaluation suggests:

> By January 15, 1976, the SEA [State Education Agency]
> ought to respond in writing to these recommendations, spel-
> ling out its specific plans and timetable for implementation.[12]

The Form to Use

Beyond developing thoughtful recommendations, it is also important to present them in a form consistent with the norms of the
sponsoring agency. For example, the evaluation of school accountability by the Florida legislature was released as a staff report,
with the committee chairman stating in the foreword that the
recommendations were staff-generated. In other situations, it
might be unacceptable for analysts to advocate particular positions
in a final report. One alternative is to put the recommendations in
an "if-then" form. For example, the recommendations of the
Connecticut evaluation of compensatory education include:

> If the legislature wants . . . [the program] to concentrate
> services primarily on low-income pupils, as the law now
> says, the statute should be amended to define "primarily" as
> meaning "80 percent of all children served, as measured by
> objective low-income criteria. . . ."
>
> If the legislature wants . . . [the program] to be something
> extra on top of regular program expenses, the law should be
> amended to require comparability of local expenditures.
> . . .[13]

Here the staff report sidesteps the value choice about what should be done, but says how to proceed once the choice is made.

Another alternative is to have the report released as an official report of the sponsoring agency, rather than as a staff document. In both the Connecticut financial aid and special education evaluations, the staff reports became the property of the subcommittee, which in turn reported to the full committee, which in turn released the reports to the public. This not only gave the legislators a sense of participation and ownership, but motivated them to become acquainted with the program, the findings, and the suggested alternatives.

III. Evaluation Standards

Currently, there are no agreed-upon standards for judging fieldwork reports. This is not surprising, given the newness of applying fieldwork methods to program evaluation. But in my view, a first-rate evaluation is valid, trustworthy, fair, well written, and useful. This is a tentative list, designed to stimulate discussion on an important subject rather than to prescribe indisputable standards carved in stone.[14] These standards, each discussed below, represent ideals. For the harried analyst facing a tight deadline, they are goals to think about, if not achieve. When you have something to say after months of investigation, it is worth trying to say it well.

A Valid Report

Much of this book concerns providing valid answers to evaluation questions. A valid report largely results from attention to procedure, and has four characteristics. First, the report is *accurate*. It reports evidence that has been collected and verified by the analyst. By guarding against observer bias, cross-checking answers, corroborating data, using several methods to collect information, sharing drafts with the host agency, and checking procedures and biases with colleagues, you substantially increase accuracy in the collection of individual bits of data.[15]

Second, the conclusions are *sound*. They are grounded in verified evidence and reflect logical procedures for drawing inferences. By searching for contradictory evidence, examining rival explanations, and sampling carefully, you can check out hunches and reach valid conclusions about characteristics, causes, and frequencies. By choosing typical, diverse, or crucial sites, you can extrapolate in different ways from a small sample.

Third, a valid report is *insightful*. It interprets the program's significance in a rich, plausible way. It provides an accurate glimpse of what the program means to those affiliated with it. Ideally, it enhances audience understanding by drawing valuable lessons from the data. An insightful report reflects the analysts' constant concern with the questions: What do the data mean? Why are they important? What do they prove? So what? What other data do we need?

Finally, a valid report is *reasonably complete*. This doesn't mean presenting "all the facts" and all the conclusions about a program, because that is impossible. But there definitely are problems if a report leaves out key facts linking two events, overlooks a critical explanation, or misses the significance of a key occurrence to those involved.

In short, a valid report accurately and adequately depicts a program's implementation and draws defensible conclusions.

A Trustworthy Report

Just because a report is valid, it doesn't necessarily follow that it will be trustworthy.[16] For a variety of reasons, the reader might not believe what he reads. A good analyst responds to this potential problem by anticipating the questions that a typical skeptical reader might want answered. The questions are similar to those raised in evaluating the credibility of a subject's account (see Chapter 3). Affirmative answers to the following nine questions will greatly increase the chances that the report's findings will be trusted. They are especially important when you are presenting controversial conclusions.

Is the report plausible? For a report to be trustworthy, it has to make sense to the reader and come across as reasonable and logical. If the results defy common sense, as is sometimes the case, the report should anticipate this reaction, acknowledge it, and buttress the conclusions with explanatory data.

Is the report coherent? It is not enough for individual bits of data to be credible; all of the pieces of the report need to fit together, to add up. A trustworthy report is internally consistent; the facts, meanings, and conclusions corroborate one another.

Do the facts in the report correspond to known facts? An obvious incorrect date, misspelled name, or mistaken title will often be enough to make the reader suspicious. If you are careless about straightforward details, the reader will wonder about carelessness in important parts of the analysis. Of course, for those readers familiar with program details, trustworthiness will depend on how well the reported detail matches the program in practice. If the reader doesn't "see" the program in the description (albeit from a different angle), he won't believe the report.

Is the report adequately documented? A report filled with un-substantiated assertions lacks credibility. If your conclusions go beyond what your data support, or if you draw substantial conclusions without presenting evidence, the report's trustworthiness will be undermined. The appropriate amount and distribution of evidence is, of course, a matter of judgment; every assertion need not be buttressed by data in the text. But trustworthiness can be enhanced by ample quotations from documents, key figures, or program clients. Integrate the quotes into the text to illustrate in concrete terms exactly what happened.

Did the analysts consult with known experts? In virtually every policy area, there are individuals and organizations that are recognized as experts—those with knowledge, experience, and a record of performance. The skeptical reader will look for evidence that such experts were consulted during the evaluation and that their views were carefully considered.

Are the analysts independent? If the evaluation is conducted by analysts with a stake in certain results, the reader will be suspicious when, lo and behold, the results match these expectations. This is a problem mainly for evaluators whose bosses are predisposed toward certain results, and for projects that use their own employees as evaluators. If independence is likely to be an issue, spell out the steps taken to minimize bias and to insure your autonomy.

Do the analysts take into account alternative interpretations? The skeptical reader is wary of a report presented as *the* story. Complicated bodies of data are always open to multiple interpretations; good analysts present their conclusions as plausible or probable, not as the only possible ones. Moreover, it is good practice to provide space (usually in the appendix) for the host agency to react to the evaluation and to offer counterinterpretations.

Are the analysts straightforward about the evaluation's limitations? The skeptical reader doesn't expect you to dissect in detail every imperfection in the evaluation, any more than you are expected to do that with the program being evaluated. But a good report is honest about data collection difficulties, possible sources of bias, and what is known with what level of certainty. The result might be a less authoritative-sounding report that catches fewer headlines, but candor can help achieve greater credibility.

Did the analyst use sound procedures? If the reader is uncertain about the report's findings, he may turn to the discussion of methodology for reassurance. A credible statement about procedures encourages the skeptical reader to give the analyst the benefit of a doubt. Consequently, the report should contain a section describing data collection procedures and the steps taken to reduce bias and error.

[174]

A Fair Report

An evaluation can have a chilling effect on a program, its personnel, and clientele. It can cause embarrassment, expose secrets, violate privacy, and destroy reputations. Because of this, you are responsible for treating both individuals and institutions fairly. At the same time, you are responsible to the report's sponsors, the public, and the program's clientele for telling the unvarnished truth. You are also responsible for conducting the evaluation in an ethical manner. Sometimes these demands conflict. If so, which parties have what rights and responsibilities? Just what does "fair" mean? What is ethical behavior?

The answers are uncertain and still evolving. Increasingly, laws are being passed to insure privacy for citizens and to protect human subjects who participate in research. For example, federally funded research projects must now go through strict clearance procedures to protect individuals from harm. At the same time, laws are being passed circumscribing the privacy of both public officials (for example, disclosure of net worth) and public agencies (for example, the federal Freedom of Information Act). For the program analyst, who deals with citizens and public officials alike, these developments suggest further questions. Do public officials have any rights as private citizens? Do private citizens benefiting from a public program give up any rights? Where do the analyst's responsibilities lie?

These questions undoubtedly will be debated for years to come. The most that is possible is to suggest emerging standards that seem relatively clear at the extremes. Consider an evaluation involving the collection of information from citizens who happen to be knowledgeable about the program, such as next-door neighbors to a state-supported housing project. As private citizens not directly benefiting from the program, they have the right to informed consent; that is, to know what their participation will involve, how long it will take, and what the potential harm may be. They can refuse to participate, or cease to participate at any time, and expect their words to be held in confidence, if that is part of the agreement. Analysts have the duty to honor these rights and to protect private citizens from direct harm resulting from the evaluation. On the other hand, you are not responsible for protecting private citizens from indirect harm growing out of program changes based on evaluation findings.

At the other extreme, consider an evaluation focusing on the activities of top public officials in institutions responsible for the operation of a program. Public institutions and officials are publicly accountable for their public action. They are not entitled to withhold participation in an authorized evaluation, nor are they entitled to have their views and activities held in confidence. Stated differently, it is appropriate to badger public officials to cooperate, if need be, and to quote them by name in the final report.

But when does badgering raise ethical dilemmas? In earlier chapters, I've discussed veiled threats, rummaging through official files, and examining personal documents. When, if ever, is it ethical to distort or omit the truth? To lie? To invade privacy? To trick your subject? These are complicated issues on which reasonable people differ. In my view, subterfuge and deceit should not be used to obtain information. An exception may occur when all other remedies have been exhausted, the data are of prime importance to the report, and the subject is a public official who is clearly accountable in the given situation. But such statements take you only so far—it is difficult to talk about ethical decisions in the absence of concrete facts and tradeoffs. Even though there are no easy answers to ethical questions, the analyst is obliged to try to come to grips with them.[17]

In between the private citizen and the top public official, there are a variety of individuals who have fewer rights than the former and more rights than the latter such as a teacher in a state-funded project, a Medicare recipient, a low-level public official. In these cases, what is appropriate and ethical is even less clear.

Regardless of the subject's status, however, you have several additional responsibilities. First, you must honor your pledges of confidentiality. But as discussed in Chapter 2, it is possible that your notes and tapes could be subpoenaed. And if your evaluation is federally funded, your confidential material might be made public under the Freedom of Information Act unless precautions are taken. At a minimum, carefully consider the possible consequences of promising confidentiality and maintain tight control over your confidential material.

Second, avoid gratuitous quotations or details in the text that only cause harm to individuals. It is inappropriate to quote a top official on an irrelevant point if its only purpose is to cause embarrassment. Third, it is usually inappropriate to identify, especially in a negative way, a public official who provided information but wasn't responsible for the identified problems. The purpose of the evaluation is not to wreck careers, but to provide a reasonably balanced picture. Finally, you should at least think about the potential misuse of the report's findings. The truth can be presented in many ways, and some are less subject than others to having the facts taken out of context and used for unintended purposes.

In short, tell the truth, but play fair. Even though the standards are unclear, a good report reflects a grappling with these issues.

A Well-Written Report

If the report is valid, trustworthy, and fair, but the prose is turgid, fuzzy, and dull, only your most doting relatives will try to beat their way through the entire document. This can be an especially serious problem if you are concerned that people understand subtle arguments. It is impossible to explore good writing in detail here, but it is possible to suggest some important features.

Simple and jargon free   Write a report in language that is understandable to the nonexpert, to someone not steeped in the special lingo of the program or profession. This rule extends to your discussion of procedures used in conducting the evaluation;

translate complicated methods into clear simple sentences. Accomplishing this is difficult, one reason why it is not often done.

Clean   By clean, I mean clear, uncluttered prose. Use words precisely. Use concrete examples abundantly. Be sure each sentence crisply conveys its meaning.

Well organized   A common fault is for a report to drone on and on, without clearly spelling out the main findings or grouping them into understandable categories. For the reader, the undifferentiated mass is too much to handle. In contrast, a well-organized report presents the material in manageable chunks that are carefully grouped, logically ordered, clearly marked, and labeled as to their importance. The reader can quickly grasp the main points and knows where the report is heading; often he is aided at the beginning by a written road map of what is to follow. Leonardo da Vinci's painting, *The Last Supper*, shows what an impact good organization can have—true in writing as well as art. Da Vinci's problem was to present the twelve apostles and Christ in a way that would quickly convey the presence of thirteen people. His solution was to group them into manageable numbers, four clusters of three apostles, with Christ in the middle. The viewer immediately grasps da Vinci's message. This is also the aim of good evaluation.

Interconnected   Think of each sentence and each paragraph as an island and of the reader as a nonswimmer. If the islands are not connected by a bridge, if there is no transition, the nonswimmer will not cross the water. Program evaluations often move from point to point without rhyme or reason. A busy reader gives up and moves to something else.

Responsive   A good writer anticipates questions and responds by building answers into the text. He does this by constantly putting himself in the place of his expected readers, and trying to explain things to *their* satisfaction, not his.

Lively   We all know that good government prose is formal and dull. "I," "you," and a telling anecdote are out. "The author," "the reader," and bloodless analysis are in. Nonsense. A sound report need not be lifeless. Just as a gourmet chef uses spice and variety, so should you. An informal tone, short sentences mixed with long, nifty quotations, apt analogies, surprising twists, and funny details can add flavor to an evaluation, if used in moderation. A good evaluation is not a novel, but it need not be a stuffy tome lulling your readers to sleep.[18]

A Useful Report

The conditions under which evaluations have a direct impact on program decisions are not well understood, and many factors are outside your control (for example, political considerations, competing sources of information). But as I have argued throughout, a focus on the hows and whys of program operations can increase the chances that the evaluation will be useful. Practical analysis and suggestions can give policymakers data and ideas to act on.

Moreover, there are several things to do to help insure utility. First, you have to meet deadlines. If the report is finished after decisions are made, the analysis obviously won't be of much use. Schedules need to be established and followed.

Second, you need to conduct the evaluation in a manner that does not embarrass or discredit your sponsors, or unduly alienate program officials. Frequent contact with key agency staff will help reduce rumors and unfair criticism of the evaluation process. Resisting media requests for data prior to the report's completion will enhance your credibility. Procedures that are efficient, respectful of those interrogated, and discreet will keep the focus on the final product, not on the process of collecting the data.

Finally, the evaluation must respond to the needs of its main audiences. Their concerns must be covered in sufficient scope; workable and appealing recommendations must be provided. To insure this fit, touch base regularly with key sponsors of the evaluation. Besides keeping the report on target, this contact can help develop their sense of ownership. This, too, will enhance the chances that the report actually will be used to alter policy.

[179]

In sum, a first-rate report is accurate, sound in conclusion, insightful, and reasonably complete. It impresses the reader as plausible, coherent, factual, adequately documented, sensitive to different interpretations, and straightforward about its limitations. It comes across as the product of independent evaluators who rely on sound procedures, and who balance their competing responsibilities to the public, their sponsors, private citizens, public officials, and program clients. In addition, the ideal report is simple, jargon free, well organized, interconnected, and responsive, and is written in clean, lively prose. The evaluation is discreetly conducted, finished on time, and marked by sensible recommendations. Putting together such an ideal report is no mean achievement. But a well-researched field evaluation could help improve the delivery of government services. The task is worth the effort.

Notes

INTRODUCTION

1. Martin Rein and Sheldon H. White, "Can Policy Research Help Policy?" *Public Interest,* vol. 49, Fall 1977, p. 119. *See also* General Accounting Office, *Status and Issues: Federal Program Evaluation,* Washington, D. C. General Accounting Office, October 1978, p. 8.

2. *See Evaluation Quarterly* (Beverly Hills, Calif.: Sage Publications); *Evaluation* (Minneapolis, Minn.: Minneapolis Medical Research Foundation, Inc.); and "How to Evaluate Education Programs: A Monthly Guide To Methods and Ideas That Work," (Washington, D.C.: Capitol Publications, Inc.).

3. Jerome T. Murphy, "The Education Bureaucracies Implement Novel Policy: The Politics of ESEA, 1965-1972," *Policy and Politics in America,* ed. Allan P. Sindler (Boston: Little, Brown, 1973).

4. Milbrey Wallin McLaughlin, "Implementation As Mutual Adaptation," *Teachers College Record,* vol. 77, no. 3, February, 1976.

5. Murphy, p. 174.

6. For a further elaboration of this argument, *see* Robert S. Weiss and

Martin Rein, "The Evaluation of Broad-Aimed Programs," in *Evaluating Action Programs,* ed. Carol Weiss (Boston: Allyn and Bacon, 1972), pp. 236-249.

7. This assumes that the major purpose of evaluation is to generate valid data that will be directly useful in making policy decisions. There is debate on this point. Some argue that the major purpose of evaluation is to affect decisions indirectly by influencing the conversation about a particular policy. *See* David K. Cohen and Michael S. Garet, "Reforming Educational Policy with Applied Research," *Harvard Educational Review,* vol. 45, no. 1, February, 1975, pp. 17-43; Carol H. Weiss, "Research For Policy's Sake: The Enlightenment Function of Social Research," *Policy Analysis,* vol. 3, no. 4, Fall 1977, pp. 531-545; and Rein and White, pp. 119-136. Also, others argue that analytic understanding is not the only road to solving social problems and improving government programs. *See* Charles E. Lindblom and David K. Cohen, *Usable Knowledge: Social Science and Social Problem Solving* (New Haven, Conn.: Yale University Press, 1979). I am basically sympathetic with these views, but this introductory text is not the place to deal with complex issues of evaluation utilization or the determinants of social problem solving.

8. There are some excellent books on evaluation, but they are oriented toward experimental design and statistical techniques. *See* Carol H. Weiss, *Evaluation Research* (Englewood Cliffs, N.J.: Prentice-Hall, 1972); and Henry Hatry et al., *Practical Program Evaluation for State and Local Government Officials* (Washington, D.C.: The Urban Institute, 1973).

There is also some excellent material on fieldwork methods, but it is geared toward long-term research rather than evaluation and tends to be designed for sociologists or anthropologists. *See* Robert Bogdan and Stephen J. Taylor, *Introduction to Qualitative Research Methods* (New York: Wiley, 1975); Jack D. Douglas, *Investigative Social Research* (Beverly Hills, Calif.: Sage, 1976); John Lofland, *Analyzing Social Settings* (Belmont, Calif.: Wadsworth, 1971); George J. McCall and J. L. Simmons, eds., *Issues in Participant Observation* (Reading, Mass.: Addison-Wesley, 1969);

and Leonard Schatzman and Anselm L. Strauss, *Field Research* (Englewood Cliffs, N.J.: Prentice-Hall, 1974). For a practical guide to ethnographic research in urban schools *see* Joan Cassell, *A Fieldwork Manual for Studying Desegregated Schools* (Washington, D.C.: National Institute of Education, September, 1978).

Several recent books on qualitative evaluation offer justifications for the approach and examples of the products that result. However, they don't deal systematically with the problems and procedures in using fieldwork methods, nor do they focus on government programs. *See* David Hamilton et al., eds., *Beyond the Numbers Game* (Berkeley: McCutchan, 1977); and George Willis, ed., *Qualitative Evaluation* (Berkeley: McCutchan, 1978).

Finally, for an excellent discussion of the "issues that fall somewhere between the poles of epistemology and technique" *see* Egon G. Guba, *Toward a Methodology of Naturalistic Inquiry in Educational Evaluation* (Los Angeles: Center for the Study of Evaluation, University of California, 1978), p. 20.

CHAPTER 1: THE EVALUATION QUESTIONS

1. Carl E. Van Horn, "Studying Policy Implementation," paper read at the American Political Science Association, February 1976.

2. For further elaboration on the subject of goals, *see* Carol H. Weiss, *Evaluation Research* (Englewood Cliffs, N.J.: Prentice-Hall, 1972), pp. 24-31; and Henry Hatry et al., *Practical Program Evaluation for State and Local Government Officials* (Washington, D.C.: Urban Institute, 1973), pp. 23-38.

3. For a provocative discussion of the meaning of success, *see* Eleanor Farrar et al., "View from Below: Implementation Research in Education," photocopied (Cambridge, Mass.: the Huron Institute, April 1979).

4. Huron Institute, "Learning From Experience," photocopied (Cambridge, Mass.: The Huron Institute, August 31, 1976), pp. 24-25.

5. Joint Committee on Education, *Schoolmen and the Poor* (Hartford, Conn.: Connecticut General Assembly, August 31, 1975), p. 4.

6. Joint Committee on Education, *Special Education: Out-of-District Placement of Exceptional Children* (Hartford, Conn.: Connecticut General Assembly, October 1975), pp. 8-9.

7. For further elaboration on indicators, *see* Weiss, pp. 34-42.

8. For further elaboration on these points, *see* Guba, *Toward a Methodology*, pp. 42-53.

9. For some interesting discussion of various models, *see* Weiss and Rein, "The Evaluation of Broad-Aimed Programs"; Graham T. Allison, *Essence of Decision* (Boston: Little, Brown, 1971); Richard F. Elmore, "Organizational Models of Social Program Implementation," *Public Policy*, vol. 26, no. 2, Spring 1978, pp. 185-228; and Van Horn.

10. Committee on Education, *Florida Education Accountability* (Tallahassee, Fla.: Florida House of Representatives, March 23, 1976), p. 9.

11. Joint Committee on Education, *Special Education*, p. 25.

12. Committee on Education, *Florida Education Accountability*, p. 57.

13. Ibid., p. 28.

14. Joint Committee on Education, *Schoolmen and the Poor*, pp. 31, 33.

15. Special Committee on Education Program Review, *Review of the Department of Public Instruction's Special Education Needs Program* (Madison, Wis.: Wisconsin Legislature, June 1976), p. S-2.

16. For both the quote and discussion of the standard, *see* Huron Institute, pp. 15-16.

17. Joint Committee on Education, *Special Education*, p. 25.

18. Joint Committee on Education, *Schoolmen and the Poor*, p. 14.

19. Committee on Education, *Florida Education Accountability*, p. 70.

CHAPTER 2: OFF AND RUNNING

1. Joint Committee on Education, *Connecticut Program of Student Financial Assistance* (Hartford, Conn.: Connecticut General Assembly, January 1976).

2. Jack De Sanctis, Unpublished field notes, Summer 1975.

3. For a further discussion of this point *see* Egon G. Guba, *Toward A Methodology of Naturalistic Inquiry in Educational Evaluation* (Los Angeles: Center for the Study of Evaluation, University of California, 1978), pp. 28-30, 67-70.

4. It should be noted that criteria other than those discussed in the text can be used in selecting sites, depending upon other possible purposes of the evaluation. For example, if an evaluation's goal is to compare impact in similar sites (such as small rural hospitals), sites would be chosen based on their common characteristics. Or a study might concentrate on "model" sites to demonstrate the most that can be reasonably expected from a program. The criteria discussed in the text, however, are among the most important and require the most elaboration. *See also,* on credibility in site selection, Seymour Sudman, *Applied Sampling* (New York: Academic Press, 1976), particularly Chapter 2.

5. Committee on Education, *Florida Educational Accountability* (Tallahassee, Fla.: Florida House of Representatives, March 23, 1976).

6. Joint Committee on Education, *Schoolmen And The Poor* (Hartford, Conn.: Connecticut General Assembly, August 31, 1975), p. 7.

7. Ibid., pp. 7, 41.

8. The material in this section on crucial sites is adapted from Harry Eckstein, "Case Study and Theory in Political Science," in *Policy and Policymaking, Handbook of Political Science* (Reading, Mass.: Addison-Wesley, 1975), Chapter 3. The analysis was also influenced by G. Polya, *Patterns of Plausible Inference, Volume II*

of Mathematics and Plausible Reasoning (Princeton, N.J.: Princeton University Press, 1954).

9. If time permits, it often pays to establish a panel of reputable, knowledgeable individuals to advise you on your samples. Following their advice can add to a sample's believability.

10. Much has been written by sociologists on the problems of entry. *See* John M. Johnson, *Doing Field Research* (New York: Free Press, 1975); George J. McCall and J. L. Simmons, eds., *Issues in Participant Observation* (Reading, Mass.: Addison-Wesley, 1969); Leonard Schatzman and Anselm L. Strauss, *Field Research* (Englewood Cliffs, N.J.: Prentice-Hall, 1974); and W. Richard Scott, "Field Methods in the Study of Organizations," in *Handbook of Organizations,* James March, ed., (Chicago: Rand McNally, 1965).

11. This happened with a study of the administration of ESEA Title I; the evaluation was sponsored by the National Institute of Education. For an interesting discussion of the issues, and another example of the use of The Freedom of Information Act to disclose confidential information, *see* L. Harmon Zeigler and Lloyd DuVall, "Freedom of Information Act and Social Science Research," American Educational Research Association Meetings (Toronto, Canada; March 27-31, 1978).

12. Another law affecting federally funded studies is the National Research Act, which is designed to protect human subjects from risk in the conduct of research. If your evaluation is federally funded, you will be required to receive clearance from an Institutional Review Board. For more details on this law, The Freedom of Information Act, and other federal statutes affecting federally funded projects, *see* Arturo Gándara, *Major Federal Regulations Governing Social Science Research* (Santa Monica, Calif.: Rand Corporation, March 1978).

As to procedures for protecting confidential material under The Freedom of Information Act, "[a federal contractor] might reconsider whether to supply its records to a federal agency or whether it should limit the information collected if it is to be shared with a federal agency" (Gándara, p. 30).

Moreover, some researchers take the further step of expunging from their files any material that might identify individuals or institutions promised confidentiality. This is well illustrated in a study done by the Survey Research Center (Institute for Social Research, University of Michigan) for the National Commission for the Protection of Human Subjects of Biomedical and Behavioral Research. The research center reported:

> The standard procedures regarding confidentiality include instructing each interviewer of the importance of maintaining the confidentiality of the data they were collecting, consistent with a long-standing policy of The Survey Research Center. . . .
>
> A number of additional steps were taken to protect the confidentiality of respondents. First, the cover sheet used by the interviewer to identify and locate the designated respondent was removed from the questionnaire as soon as it arrived at the Center. The cover sheet was then filed separately in a locked cabinet. Some information from the cover sheet and the project information form was coded, . . . However, no names were coded or entered into the data files. The cover sheet and project information forms were then destroyed.
>
> Second, names of persons, institutions, and drugs and certain items of demographic information about respondents were physically cut out of completed questionnaires and destroyed. Some of these items of information, such as age or title of respondent, were coded into relatively broad categories.
>
> Third, the sample books and numerical logging materials used in accounting for sample projects were kept in a locked vault after normal working hours. The control clerk assigned to the study had a list of persons who were allowed access to these books. The names of principal investigators and the names of their projects have now been physically cut out of the sample books and destroyed. Before the final report or any data tapes are released from The Survey Record Center, the sample books will be destroyed.
>
> Fourth, the consent forms and the first two pages of each questionnaire, which contain descriptions of the projects, were stored in Canada. The identifying numbers that connect

the data in the tapes with specific questionnaires were scrambled. Additionally, the address labels prepared for all respondents (for the purpose of sending them copies of a summary report) were stored in Canada.

(The National Commission for the Protection of Human Subjects of Biomedical and Behavioral Research, *Appendix to Report and Recommendations: Institutional Review Boards* (Washington, D.C.: U.S. Department of Health, Education, and Welfare, September 1, 1978), Appendix pp. 274-275).

13. Sometimes, however, researchers resort to more underhanded tactics for getting into organizations. For a discussion of various ways to infiltrate a research site, see Jack D. Douglas, *Investigative Social Research* (Beverly Hills, Calif.: Sage, 1976).

CHAPTER 3: COPING WITH BIAS AND ERROR

1. Note that I say that the results are consistent with, not necessarily identical with, those of other investigators. In fact, because of different perspectives and other factors, different investigators may emphasize different facets of the program. A full discussion of the scientific standard of reliability or replicability and its application to fieldwork goes beyond the scope of this introductory text. The interested reader should see Egon G. Guba, *Toward a Methodology of Naturalistic Inquiry in Educational Evaluation* (Los Angeles: Center for the Study of Evaluation, University of California, 1978), pp. 70-73. Also, the issue is usefully stated by Schatzman and Strauss:

> [This] leads to another question which audiences might raise, bearing upon the repeatability or reliability of the work. Would another independent observer have seen or heard the same events, and reached the same conclusions? . . .
>
> For the field researcher whose view of social reality is one of indefinite complexity, the only germane question is, *Would an independent observer make conceptual discoveries that empirically or logically invalidate his own?* That another observer—with or without the same general framework or

perspective—might develop a very different analytic scheme, conceptual model or metaphor is to be expected. Perceptual and conceptual selectivity must be taken for granted. Some identical and some different events would become data for other field observers; therefore, all independently developed data and analyses would necessarily be different. One or another analysis may be conceptually superior, but if any fails to contradict the original research, it must be regarded as supplementary or complementary. [Emphasis in original]

(Leonard Schatzman and Anselm L. Strauss, *Field Research* (Englewood Cliffs, N.J.: Prentice-Hall, 1973), p. 134.)

2. For a more detailed discussion of various sources of bias and error, *see* Jack D. Douglas, *Investigative Social Research* (Beverly Hills, Calif.: Sage, 1976); Raymond L. Gordon, *Interviewing* (Homewood, Ill.: Dorsey, 1975); Guba, ibid.; John Lofland, *Analyzing Social Settings* (Belmont, Calif.: Wadsworth, 1971); George J. McCall and J. L. Simmons, eds., *Issues in Participant Observation* (Reading, Mass.: Addison-Wesley, 1969); Schatzman and Strauss, ibid.; W. Richard Scott, "Field Methods in The Study of Organizations," in *Handbook of Organizations,* ed. James G. March (Chicago: Rand McNally, 1965); M. D. Shipman, *The Limitations of Social Research* (London: Longman, 1972); Eugene J. Webb et al., *Unobtrusive Measures* (Chicago: Rand McNally, 1966); and Jacqueline P. Wiseman, "The Research Web," *Urban Life and Culture,* vol. 3, no. 3 (October 1974).

3. Abraham Kaplan, *The Conduct of Inquiry* (San Francisco: Chandler, 1964), p. 28.

4. John M. Johnson, *Doing Field Research* (New York: Free Press, 1975), pp. 152-153.

5. Francis L. Wellman, *The Art of Cross-Examination* (New York: Collier, 1936), p. 162.

6. Ibid., p. 173.

7. For a more detailed discussion of subject (un)cooperation, *see* Jack D. Douglas, *Investigative Social Research* (Beverly Hills, Calif.: Sage, 1976), Chapter 4.

8. For a more detailed discussion of the various categories of problems lumped under the heading "reactivity," *see* Webb et al.

9. Quoted in McCall and Simmons, p. 269.

10. Some of these tests were adapted from James G. March, "Analytic Skills and the University Training of Educational Administrators," *Education and Urban Society,* vol. 6, 1973-74, pp. 382-427.

11. For a detailed discussion of the need for triangulation, *see* Webb et al.

Chapter 4: Intensive Interviewing

1. My thinking for this chapter was influenced by a number of writings, most notably Robert Bogdan and Steven J. Taylor, *Introduction to Qualitative Research Methods* (New York: Wiley, 1975); John Brady, *The Craft of Interviewing* (Cincinnati: Writer's Digest, 1976); Charles F. Cannell and Robert L. Kahn, "Interviewing," in *The Handbook of Social Psychology,* 2nd ed., Gardner Lindzey and Elliot Aronson, eds. (Reading, Mass.: Addison-Wesley, 1968); Lewis Anthony Dexter, *Elite and Specialized Interviewing* (Evanston, Ill.: Northwestern University Press, 1970); Jack D. Douglas, *Investigative Social Research* (Beverly Hills, Calif.: Sage, 1976); Raymond L. Gordon, *Interviewing,* rev. ed. (Homewood, Ill.: Dorsey, 1975); John Lofland, *Analyzing Social Settings* (Belmont, Calif.: Wadsworth, 1971); Leonard Schatzman and Anselm L. Strauss, *Field Research* (Englewood Cliffs, N.J.: Prentice-Hall, 1974); and W. Richard Scott, "Field Methods in The Study of Organizations," in *Handbook of Organizations*, James G. March, ed. (Chicago: Rand McNally, 1965).

2. Carl E. Van Horn, "Studying Policy Implementation," paper read at the American Political Science Association, February, 1976.

3. Ralph Craft, *Legislative Follow-Through* (New Brunswick, N.J.: Eagleton Institute, Rutgers University, 1977), p. 10.

4. Brady, p. 160.

5. Dexter, p. 59.

6. Brady, p. 52.

CHAPTER 5: TRANSIENT OBSERVATION AND DOCUMENT ANALYSIS

1. For further elaboration on participant observation, *see* Robert Bogdan and Steven J. Taylor, *Introduction to Qualitative Research Methods* (New York: Wiley, 1975); John Lofland, *Analyzing Social Settings* (Belmont, Calif.: Wadsworth, 1971); George J. McCall and J. L. Simmons, eds., *Issues in Participant Observation* (Reading, Mass.: Addison-Wesley, 1969); Leonard Schatzman and Anselm L. Strauss, *Field Research* (Englewood Cliffs, N.J.: Prentice-Hall, 1974).

Another variety of participant observation, popular in social science as well as in police work and journalism, is the disguised observer. For example, social scientists disguised themselves as patients to study the hospital treatment of the insane. In Washington, D.C., and elsewhere, police have set up phony fencing operations to lure thieves into their net. In Chicago, a newspaper bought a bar and staffed it with two reporters to trap fire and building-safety inspectors who were taking bribes.

This approach offers access to information that might be unavailable any other way, and eliminates major biases caused by the researcher's presence. But this approach, besides being quite time-consuming, can also raise serious ethical and legal questions. It also hamstrings the observer; he can't ask research-like questions or move about freely without blowing his cover. For all these reasons, this role is inappropriate in the type of government program evaluation discussed here. (The pseudo-patient example was cited in Sissela Bok, *Lying* (New York: Pantheon, 1978), pp. 197-198. The Washington, D.C. and Chicago examples were reported on national television in 1977 and 1978.)

2. The term "transient observation" is adopted from Scott who used

the terms "transitory" and "sustained" observation to highlight one dimension along which observational studies differ. *See* W. Richard Scott, "Field Methods in The Study of Organizations," in *Handbook of Organizations,* James G. March, ed. (Chicago: Rand McNally, 1965), pp. 261-304.

It should be noted that *disguised* transient observers have been used by legislative bodies as part of their oversight activities. For example, Congressional staff have posed as Medicaid patients to uncover fraudulent practices. Such undercover investigative procedures are beyond the scope of this book. (*See* Sissela Bok, *Lying,* pp. 198-199.)

3. For some examples of provocative, if not particularly scholarly, discussion of nonverbal behavior, *see* Julius Fast, *Body Language* (New York: Pocket Books, 1971); Desmond Morris, *Manwatching* (New York: Abrams, 1977); and Gerard I. Nierenberg and Henry H. Calero, *How to Read a Person Like a Book* (New York: Pocket Books, 1973).

4. This notice was found during a visit to the Colorado State Department of Education in December, 1971.

5. This story was found during a visit to the Colorado State Department of Education in July, 1976.

6. The term "unobtrusive measures" comes from Eugene J. Webb et al., *Unobtrusive Measures* (Chicago: Rand McNally, 1966). In addition, my discussion (and examples) were obviously influenced by this book.

7. For further elaboration on field notes, see Bogdan and Taylor; Lofland; and Schatzman and Strauss.

8. For further elaboration on document analysis, *see* Bill Burges, *You Can Look It Up* (Boston: Institute for Responsive Education, 1976); Barney G. Glaser and Anselm L. Strauss, *The Discovery of Grounded Theory* (Chicago: Aldine, 1967); Scott, *Field Methods;* Alden Todd, *Finding Facts Fast* (New York: Morrow, 1972); and Carol H. Weiss, *Evaluation Research* (Englewood Cliffs, N.J.: Prentice-Hall, 1972).

9. The paper example comes from Donald H. Graves, "We Won't Let Them Write" (Durham, N.H.: University of New Hampshire, xeroxed, January 1977). The Irish example comes from Peter Schrag, *Village School Downtown* (Boston: Beacon, 1967).

10. From Graham T. Allison, *Essence of Decision* (Boston: Little, Brown, 1971), p. 181.

11. But with the increasing access to public records through public information laws, like the federal Freedom of Information Act, I suspect that more government business transpires orally and even internal documents are being written with an eye toward their eventual public consumption. Nonetheless, they can be quite helpful.

12. Joint Committee on Education, *Special Education: Out-of-District Placement of Exceptional Children* (Hartford, Conn.: Connecticut General Assembly, October 1975), p. 61.

13. Joint Committee on Education, *Schoolmen and the Poor* (Hartford, Conn.: Connecticut General Assembly, August 31, 1975), pp. 6-7.

14. George Meier, Staff, Committee on Education, Florida House of Representatives, 1976.

CHAPTER 6: ANALYZING AND WRITING

1. Jacqueline P. Wiseman, "The Research Web," *Urban Life and Culture,* vol. 3, no. 3 (October 1974), p. 317.

2. John R. Trimble, *Writing With Style* (Englewood Cliffs, N.J.: Prentice-Hall, 1975), pp. 38-39.

3. From P. W. Bridgman, in Abraham Kaplan, *The Conduct of Inquiry* (San Francisco: Chandler, 1964), p. 27. Readers interested in aggregating data from many case studies should see William A. Lucas, *The Case Survey Method* (Santa Monica, Calif.: Rand, October 1974), and Robert K. Yin et al., *A Review of Case Studies of Technological Innovations in State and Local Services,* (Santa Monica, Calif.: Rand Corporation, February 1976).

4. I have excluded propositions involving correlations (for example, the more supportive the teachers, the happier the students) because they are not normally examined in fieldwork and because their proper testing requires quantitative analysis that is beyond the scope of this book.

5. For a more detailed discussion of causation, *see* particularly Donald T. Campbell and Julian C. Stanley, *Experimental and Quasi-Experimental Design for Research* (Chicago: Rand Mc-Nally, 1966); and John Lofland, *Analyzing Social Settings* (Belmont, Calif.: Wadsworth, 1971).

6. For a further discussion of systematic comparison, *see* Allen H. Barton and Paul F. Lazarsfeld, "Some Functions of Qualitative Analysis in Social Research," in George J. McCall and J. L. Simmons, eds., *Issues In Participant Observation* (Reading, Mass.: Addison-Wesley, 1969), pp. 189-192.

7. For a further discussion of categorizing and types of categories, *see* Leonard Schatzman and Anselm L. Strauss, *Field Research* (Englewood Cliffs, N.J.: Prentice-Hall, 1973), pp. 110-117; Barton and Lazarsfeld, pp. 173-182; and Egon G. Guba, *Toward a Methodology of Naturalistic Inquiry in Educational Evaluation* (Los Angeles: Center for the Study of Evaluation, University of California, 1978), pp. 49-61.

8. For a discussion of coding procedures, *see* Wiseman; the introduction in William L. Howarth, ed., *The John McPhee Reader* (New York: Vintage, 1977); and Joan Cassell, *A Fieldwork Manual for Studying Desegregated Schools* (Washington, D.C.: National Institute of Education, September 1978), pp. 50-52.

9. For a further elaboration, *see* Kate L. Turabian, *Student's Guide For Writing College Papers* (Chicago: University of Chicago, 1976), pp. 41-44. *See also* Carolyn J. Mullins, *A Guide to Writing and Publishing in the Social and Behavioral Sciences* (New York: Wiley, 1977).

10. The content of this section was influenced by a number of writings. Particularly, *see* John Lofland, *Analyzing Social Settings* (Belmont, Calif.: Wadsworth, 1971); Wiseman; Trimble; and Howarth.

11. Susan Moore Johnson, unpublished paper, Spring 1977.

12. From newsletter of Center for Creative Leadership, vol. 5, no. 1 (Greensboro, N.C., February 1978), p. 3.

13. Trimble, p. 95.

14. Walter E. Allen, ed., *Writers on Writing* (London: Phoenix, 1948), p. 65.

15. The material on Kant and Schiller came from James L. Adams, *Conceptual Blockbusting* (San Francisco: Freeman, 1974), p. 44; the material on Frost and Hemingway came from Kay Dick, ed., *Writers At Work* (Harmondsworth, Eng.: Penguin, 1972), pp. 68, 176. The heading "Writer's Nest" was suggested to me by Patricia Stewart.

16. From Patricia Stewart, unpublished paper Spring 1977. The idea of writing in "takes" comes from Wiseman.

17. For a further elaboration of "working backwards," *see* G. Polya, *How to Solve It* (New York: Doubleday, 1957), pp. 225-232.

18. The books that were particularly influential in writing this section include Adams; Rollo May, *The Courage to Create* (New York: Bantam, 1975); and G. Polya, *Volumes I and II of Mathematics and Plausible Reasoning* (Princeton University Press, 1954).

CHAPTER 7: SUMMING UP
AND APPLYING STANDARDS

1. Joint Committee on Education, *Connecticut Programs of Student Financial Assistance* (Hartford, Conn.: Connecticut General Assembly, October 1975), p. 3.

2. Committee on Education, *Florida Education Accountability* (Tallahassee, Fla.: Florida House of Representatives, March 23, 1976), p. 60.

3. Joint Committee on Education, *Schoolmen and the Poor* (Hartford, Conn.: Connecticut General Assembly, August 31, 1975), p. 29.

4. Ibid., pp. 1-2.

5. For a helpful discussion of some problems of reorganization, *see* Harold Seidman, *Politics, Position and Power* (New York: Oxford, 1970). Also, for an interesting discussion of the virtues of duplication in government, *see* Martin Landau, "Redundancy, Rationality, and the Problem of Duplication and Overlap," in Francis E. Rourke, ed., *Bureaucratic Power in National Politics,* 2nd ed. (Boston: Little, Brown, 1972), pp. 337-358.

6. Joint Committee on Education, *Schoolmen and the Poor,* p. 60.

7. Committee on Education, *Florida Education Accountability,* p. xiii.

8. For a provocative discussion of the problems associated with a compliance orientation, *see* Richard F. Elmore, "Complexity and Control: What Legislators and Administrators Can Do About Implementation" (Seattle: University of Washington, Institute of Governmental Research, April 1979).

9. Joint Committee on Education, *Schoolmen and the Poor,* p. 63.

10. Committee on Education, *Florida Education Accountability,* p. xiv.

11. Joint Committee on Education, *Connecticut Programs of Student Financial Assistance,* p. 4.

12. Joint Committee on Education, *Schoolmen and the Poor,* p. 47.

13. Ibid., pp. 56, 58.

14. The general discussion of standards in this section was influenced by a number of books and papers, including Elliot W. Eisner, "Educational Connoisseurship and Educational Criticism" (Stanford, Calif.: Stanford University, © 1976); Frederick Erickson, "On Standards of Descriptive Validity in Studies of Classroom Activity" (Paper delivered at the Annual Meeting of the American Educational Research Association, Toronto, Canada, March 29, 1978); Barney G. Glaser and Anselm L. Strauss, *The Discovery of Grounded Theory* (Chicago: Aldine, 1967); Egon G. Guba, *Toward a Methodology of Naturalistic Inquiry in Educational Evaluation*

(Los Angeles: Center for the Study of Evaluation, University of California, 1978); Leonard Schatzman and Anselm L. Strauss, *Field Research* (Englewood Cliffs, N.J.: Prentice-Hall, 1974); Daniel L. Stufflebeam, *Meta-Evaluation* (Kalamazoo, Mich.: Evaluation Center, Western Michigan University, 1974); and Stufflebeam, "Overview of the Joint Committee's Project on Evaluation Standards" (Paper delivered at the Annual Meeting of the American Educational Research Association, New York, N.Y., April 5, 1977).

15. You also substantially increase the odds that if an independent investigator repeated the study, the results would be consistent. *See* note 1 in Chapter 3 for a further discussion of replicability.

16. Similarly, just because a report is trustworthy, it doesn't necessarily follow that it is valid. The report might sound right to the reader who is unfamiliar with the program, yet contain unknown inaccuracies, faulty interpretations, and outright fabrications. Thus, neither validity nor trustworthiness can stand alone as a test of a good report.

17. For interesting discussions of ethics in conducting social science, *see* Sissela Bok, *Lying* (New York: Pantheon, 1978), and Eugene J. Webb et al., *Unobtrusive Measures* (Chicago: Rand McNally, 1966).

18. In my view, the two best books on writing are William Strunk, Jr., and E. B. White, *The Elements of Style*, 2nd ed. (New York: Macmillan, 1972); and John R. Trimble, *Writing With Style* (Englewood Cliffs, N.J.: Prentice-Hall, 1975).

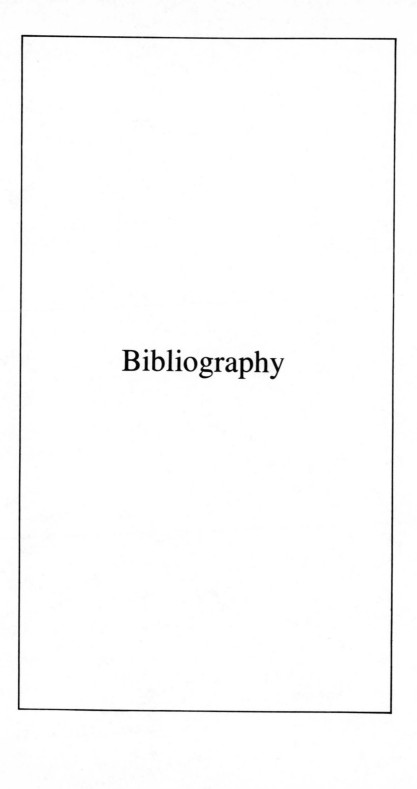

Bibliography

ADAMS, JAMES L. *Conceptual Blockbusting: A Guide to Better Ideas*. San Francisco: W. H. Freeman and Company, 1974.

ADAMS, R. N., and J. J. Preiss, eds. *Human Organization Research*. Homewood, Ill.: The Dorsey Press, Inc., 1960.

ALLEN, WALTER E., ed. *Writers on Writing*. London: Phoenix House, 1948.

ALLISON, GRAHAM T. *Essence of Decision: Explaining the Cuban Missile Crisis*. Boston: Little, Brown and Company, 1971.

ASHER, J. WILLIAM. *Educational Research and Evaluation Methods*. Boston: Little, Brown and Company, 1976.

BATES, JEFFERSON D. *Writing With Precision: How To Write So That You Cannot Possibly Be Misunderstood*. Washington, D.C.: Acropolis Books Ltd., 1978.

BERNSTEIN, CARL, AND BOB WOODWARD. *All the President's Men*. New York: Warner Books, 1975.

BLALOCK, HUBERT M., JR. *An Introduction to Social Research*. Englewood Cliffs, N.J.: Prentice-Hall, 1970.

BOGDAN, ROBERT, AND STEVEN J. TAYLOR. *Introduction To Qualitative Research Methods: A Phenomenological Approach To The Social Sciences*. New York: John Wiley and Sons, 1975.

BOK, SISSELA. *Lying: Moral Choice in Public and Private Life*. New York: Pantheon Books, 1978.

BRADY, JOHN. *The Craft of Interviewing*. Cincinnati: Writer's Digest Books, 1976.

BURGES, BILL. *Facts and Figures: A Layman's Guide To Conducting Surveys*. Boston: Institute for Responsive Education, 1976.

BURGES, BILL. *Facts For A Change*. Boston: Institute for Responsive Education, 1976.

BURGES, BILL. *You Can Look It Up: Finding Educational Documents*. Boston: Institute for Responsive Education, 1976.

BURNS, ALLAN. "An Anthropologist at Work: Field Perspectives on Applied Ethnography and an Independent Research Firm." *The Council on Anthropology and Education Quarterly*, November 1975, pp. 28–34.

CAMPBELL, DONALD T. "Qualitative Knowing in Action Research." Evanston, Ill.: Northwestern University, Kurt Lewin Award Address, Society for the Psychological Study of Social Issues, Meeting with the American Psychological Association, New Orleans, September 1, 1974.

CAMPBELL, DONALD T., AND JULIAN C. STANLEY. *Experimental and Quasi-experimental Designs for Research*. Chicago: Rand McNally, 1966.

CANNELL, CHARLES F., AND ROBERT L. KAHN. "Interviewing." In *The Handbook of Social Psychology*, edited by Gardner Lindzey and Elliot Aronson, 2nd ed. Reading, Mass.: Addison-Wesley, 1968.

CARLINI, PATRICIA F. *Observation and Description: An Alternative Methodology For The Investigation of Human Phenomena*. Grand Forks, N.D.: University of North Dakota, 1975.

CARO, FRANCIS G., ed. *Readings in Evaulation Research*. Hartford, Conn.: Russell Sage Foundation, 1971.

CASSELL, JOAN. *A Fieldwork Manual for Studying Desegregated Schools*. Washington, D.C.: The National Institute of Education, September, 1978.

CLINTON, CHARLES A. "On Bargaining with the Devil: Contract Ethnography and Accountability in Fieldwork." *The Council on Anthropology and Education Quarterly*, May 1976, pp. 25–28.

COHEN, DAVID K., AND MICHAEL S. GARET. "Reforming Educational Policy with Applied Research." *Harvard Educational Review*, vol. 45, no. 1 (February 1975), pp. 17–43.

COMMITTEE ON EDUCATION. *Florida Educational Accountability: A Program Review.* Tallahassee, Fla.: Florida House of Representatives, March 23, 1976.

COTTAM, KEITH M., AND ROBERT W. PELTON. *Writer's Research Handbook.* New York: Barnes and Noble, 1977.

DENZIN, NORMAN K. *The Research Act.* Chicago: Aldine Press, 1970.

DENZIN, NORMAN K., ed. *Sociological Methods: A Sourcebook.* New York: McGraw-Hill, 1970.

DEXTER, LEWIS ANTHONY. *Elite and Specialized Interviewing.* Evanston, Ill.: Northwestern University Press, 1970.

DICK, KAY, ed. *Writers At Work: The Paris Review Interviews.* Harmondsworth, England: Penguin, 1972.

DOUGLAS, JACK D. *Investigative Social Research: Individual and Team Field Research.* Beverly Hills, Calif.: Sage Publications, 1976.

ECKSTEIN, HARRY. "Case Study and Theory In Political Science." In *Policy and Policymaking, Handbook of Political Science.* Reading, Mass.: Addison-Wesley, 1975.

EISNER, ELLIOT W. "The Perceptive Eye: Toward the Reformation of Educational Evaluation." Invited Address, Division B Curriculum and Objectives. American Educational Research Association, Washington, D.C., March 31, 1975.

EISNER, ELLIOT W. "Educational Connoisseurship and Educational Criticism: Their Form and Functions in Educational Evaluation." Stanford, Calif.: Stanford University, Xeroxed, 1976.

ELBOW, PETER. *Writing Without Teachers.* New York: Oxford University Press, 1973.

ELMORE, RICHARD F. "Complexity and Control: What Legislators and Administrators Can Do About Implementation." Seattle, Wash.: University of Washington, Institute of Governmental Research, April 1979.

ELMORE, RICHARD F. "Organizational Models of Social Program Implementation." *Public Policy*, vol. 26, no. 2 (Spring, 1978), pp. 185–228.

ERICKSON, FREDERICK. "Some Approaches to Inquiry in School/ Community Ethnography." Paper delivered at the Workshop Exploring Qualitative/Quantitative Research Methodologies in Education, July 23, 1976.

ERICKSON, FREDERICK. "On Standards of Descriptive Validity in Studies of Classroom Activity." Paper delivered at the Annual Meeting of The American Educational Research Association, Toronto, Canada, March 29, 1978.

EVERHART, ROBERT B. "Problems of Doing Fieldwork in Educational Evaluation." *Human Organization*, vol. 34, no. 2 (Summer 1975), pp. 205–215.

FARRAR, ELEANOR; JOHN E. DE SANCTIS; AND DAVID K. COHEN. "View From Below: Implementation Research in Education." Xeroxed. Cambridge, Mass.: The Huron Institute, April 1979.

FENNO, RICHARD F., JR. *Home Style: House Members in Their Districts*. Boston: Little, Brown and Company, 1978.

FERREIRA, JOSEPH, AND BILL BURGES. *Collecting Evidence: A Layman's Guide To Participant Observation*. Boston: Institute for Responsive Education, 1976.

FILSTEAD, WILLIAM J., ed. *Qualitative Methodology: Firsthand Involvement with the Social World*. Chicago: Markham Publishing Co., 1970.

FISCHER, D. H. *Historians' Fallacies: Toward a Logic of Historical Thought*. New York: Harper and Row, 1970.

GÁNDARA, ARTURO. *Major Federal Regulations Governing Social Science Research*. Santa Monica, Calif.: Rand Corporation, March 1978.

GENERAL ACCOUNTING OFFICE. *Status and Issues: Federal Program Evaluation*. Washington, D.C.: General Accounting Office, October 1978.

GLASER, BARNEY G., AND ANSELM L. STRAUSS. *The Discovery of Grounded Theory*. Chicago: Aldine Press, 1967.

GOODLAD, JOHN, AND M. FRANCIS KLEIN. *Looking Behind the Classroom Door*. Worthington, Ohio: Charles Jones Publishing Co., 1974.

GORDON, RAYMOND L. *Interviewing: Strategy, Techniques and Tactics*. rev. ed. Homewood, Ill.: The Dorsey Press, 1975.

GUBA, EGON G. *Toward A Methodology of Naturalistic Inquiry in Educational Evaluation*. Los Angeles: Center for the Study of Evaluation, University of California, 1978.

HAMILTON, DAVID; BARRY MCDONALD; CHRISTINE KING; DAVID JENKINS; AND MALCOLM PARLETT, eds. *Beyond The Numbers Game: A Reader in Educational Evaluation*. Berkeley, Calif.: McCutchan Publishing Corporation, 1977.

HATRY, HENRY P.; RICHARD E. WINNIE; AND DONALD M. FISK. *Practical Program Evaluation for State and Local Government Officials*. Washington, D.C.: The Urban Institute, 1973.

HIRSCH, ERIC DONALD. *Validity in Interpretation*. New Haven: Yale University Press, 1967.

HOUSE, ERNEST R. *The Logic of Evaluative Argument*. Los Angeles: Center for the Study of Evaluation, University of California, 1977.

HOUSE, ERNEST R, ed *School Evaluation: The Politics and Process*. Berkeley, Calif.: McCutchan Publishing Corporation, 1972.

HOWARTH, WILLIAM L., ed. *The John McPhee Reader*. New York: Vintage Books, 1977.

HURON INSTITUTE. "Learning From Experience: A Proposal To Study The Implementation of EBCE." Xeroxed. Cambridge, Mass.: The Huron Institute, August 31, 1976.

JOHNSON, JOHN M. *Doing Field Research*. New York: The Free Press, 1975.

JOINT COMMITTEE ON EDUCATION. *Connecticut Programs of Student Financial Assistance: Final Report*. Hartford, Conn.: Connecticut General Assembly, January 1976.

JOINT COMMITTEE ON EDUCATION. *Schoolmen And The Poor: The Implementation of Connecticut's State Act For Disadvantaged Children: Final Report*. Hartford, Conn.: Connecticut General Assembly, August 31, 1975.

JOINT COMMITTEE ON EDUCATION. *Special Education: Out-of-District Placement of Exceptional Children: Final Report*. Hartford, Conn.: Connecticut General Assembly, October, 1975.

JUNKER, BUFORD. *Fieldwork: An Introduction to the Social Sciences*. Chicago: University of Chicago Press, 1960.

KAPLAN, ABRAHAM. *The Conduct of Inquiry: Methodology for Behavioral Science*. San Francisco: Chandler Publishing Company, 1964.

KATZER, JEFFREY; KENNETH H. COOK, AND WAYNE W. CROUCH. *Evaluating Information: A Guide for Users of Social Science Research*. Reading, Mass.: Addison-Wesley, 1978.

KERLINGER, FREDERICK N. *Foundations of Behavioral Research: Educational, Psychological, and Sociological Inquiry*. 2nd ed. New York: Holt, Rinehart and Winston, 1973.

KOCH, CARL, AND JAMES M. BRAZIL, eds. *Strategies For Teaching The Composition Process*. Urbana, Ill.: National Council of Teachers of English, 1978.

KUHN, THOMAS S. *The Structure of Scientific Revolutions*. Chicago, Ill.: University of Chicago Press, 1963.

LANDAU, MARTIN. "Redundancy, Rationality, and The Problem of Duplication and Overlap." In *Bureaucratic Power In National Politics*, edited by Francis E. Rourke, pp. 337-358. 2nd ed. Boston: Little, Brown and Company, 1972.

LINDBLOM, CHARLES E., AND DAVID K. COHEN. *Usable Knowledge. Social Science and Social Problem Solving*. New Haven: Yale University Press, 1979.

LOFLAND, JOHN. *Analyzing Social Settings: A Guide to Qualitative Observation and Analysis*. Belmont, Calif.: Wadsworth Publishing Co., 1971.

LUCAS, WILLIAM A. *The Case Survey Method: Aggregating Case Experience*. Santa Monica, Calif.: The Rand Corporation, October 1974.

LUTZ, FRANK W., AND LAURENCE IANNACCONE. *Understanding Educational Organizations: A Field Study Approach*. Columbus, Ohio: Charles E. Merrill, 1969.

MARCH, JAMES G. "Model Bias in Social Action." *Review of Educational Research*, vol. 42, no. 4 (February 1972), pp. 413–429.

MARCH, JAMES G. "Analytic Skills And The University Training of

Educational Administrators. "*Education and Urban Society*, vol. 6 (1973–74), pp. 382–427.

MAY, ROLLO. *The Courage To Create*. New York: Bantam Books, 1975.

McCALL, GEORGE J., AND J. L. SIMMONS; eds. *Issues in Participant Observation: A Text and Reader*. Reading, Mass.: Addison-Wesley, 1969.

McLAUGHLIN, MILBREY WALLIN. "Implementation As Mutual Adaptation: Change in Classroom Organization." *Teachers College Record*, vol. 77, no. 3 (February 1976).

MORRIS, DESMOND. *Manwatching: A Field Guide To Human Behavior*. New York: Harry N. Abrams, Inc., 1977.

MORRIS, LYNN LYONS, AND CAROL TAYLOR FITZ-GIBBON. *How to Measure Program Implementation*. Beverly Hills, Calif.: Sage Publications, 1978.

MULHAUSER, FREDERICK. "Ethnography and Policymaking: The Case of Education." *Human Organization*, vol. 34, no. 3 (Fall 1975), pp. 311–314.

MULLINS, CAROLYN J. *A Guide to Writing and Publishing in the Social and Behavioral Sciences*. New York: John Wiley and Sons, 1977.

MURPHY, JEROME T. "The Education Bureaucracies Implement Novel Policy: The Politics of ESEA, 1965–1972." In *Policy and Politics in America: Six Case Studies*, edited by Allan P. Sindler. Boston: Little, Brown and Company, 1973.

MURPHY, JEROME T. "Program Evaluations by Legislative Staff: Some Lessons Learned." A paper presented at the Annual Meeting of the American Educational Research Association, April 22, 1976.

MURPHY, JEROME T. "Musings on the Utility of Decision-making Models." *Harvard Educational Review*, vol. 47, no. 1 (November 1977), pp. 565–569.

MYATT, WILLIAM. *Stalking the Wild Semicolon*. Santa Rosa, Calif.: Thresh Publications, 1976.

O'HAYRE, JOHN. *Gobbledygook Has Gotta Go*. Washington, D.C.: U.S. Government Printing Office, undated.

PATTON, MICHAEL Q. *Alternative Evaluation Research Paradigm*. Grand Forks, N.D. University of North Dakota, 1975.

PATTON, MICHAEL Q. *Utilization—Focused Evaluation*. Beverly Hills, Calif.: Sage Publications, 1978.

PAYNE, S. L. *The Art of Asking Questions*. Princeton, N.J.: Princeton University Press, 1951.

PELTO, P. *Anthropological Research: The Structure of Inquiry*. New York: Harper and Row, 1970.

POLANYI, MICHAEL. *The Tacit Dimension*. New York: Doubleday, 1966.

POLYA, G. *Induction and Analogy in Mathematics. Volume I of Mathematics and Plausible Reasoning*. Princeton, N.J.: Princeton University Press, 1954.

POLYA, G. *Patterns of Plausible Inference. Volume II of Mathematics and Plausible Reasoning*. Princeton, N.J.: Princeton University Press, 1954.

POLYA, G. *How To Solve It*. 2nd ed. New York: Doubleday, 1957.

POWDERMAKER, HORTENSE. *Stranger and Friend: The Way of an Anthropologist*. New York: W. W. Norton & Co., 1966.

REIN, MARTIN, AND SHELDON H. WHITE. "Can Policy Research Help Policy?" *Public Interest*. vol. 49 (Fall 1977), pp. 119–136.

RIST, RAY C. "On the Relations Among Educational Research Paradigms: From Disdain to Detente." Paper delivered at the Workshop Exploring Qualitative/Quantitative Research Methodologies in Education, sponsored by NIE and the Far West Laboratory, July 23, 1976.

RIST, RAY C. "On Qualitative Research: Issues of Design, Implementation, Analysis, Ethics, and Applicability—A Bibliography." Ithaca, N.Y.: College of Human Ecology, Cornell University, 1978.

RIVLIN, ALICE M., AND MICHAEL P. TIMPANE, eds. *Planned Variation in Education: Should We Give Up or Try Harder?* Washington, D.C.: The Brookings Institute, 1975.

ROSENTHAL, ROBERT, AND RALPH L. ROSNOW. *Primer of Methods For The Behavioral Sciences*. New York: John Wiley and Sons, 1975.

Rossi, Peter M., and Walter Williams, eds. *Evaluating Social Programs: Theory, Practice and Politics*. New York: Seminar Press, 1972.

Rutman, Leonard, ed. *Evaluation Research Methods: A Basic Guide*. Beverly Hills, Calif.: Sage Publications, 1977.

Schatzman, Leonard, and Anselm L. Strauss. *Field Research: Strategies For a Natural Sociology*. Englewood Cliffs, N.J.: Prentice-Hall, 1973.

Schrag, Peter. *Village School Downtown: Politics and Education —A Boston Report*. Boston: Beacon Press, 1967.

Scott, W. Richard. "Field Methods in the Study of Organizations." In *Handbook of Organizations*, edited by James G. March, pp. 261–304. Chicago, Ill.: Rand McNally, 1965.

Seidman, Harold. *Politics, Position, and Power: The Dynamics of Federal Organization*. New York: Oxford University Press, 1970.

Shipman, M.D. *The Limitations of Social Research*. London: Longman Group Limited, 1972.

Special Committee on Education Program Review. *Review of The Department of Public Instruction's Special Education Needs Program*. Madison, Wis.: Wisconsin Legislature, June 1976.

Stake, Robert E. *Evaluating the Arts in Education: A Responsive Approach*. Columbus, Ohio: Charles E. Merrill, 1975.

Stake, Robert E. *Evaluating Educational Programs: The Need and The Response*. Paris: Organization for Economic Cooperation and Development, 1976.

Stake, Robert E. "The Case Study Method in Social Inquiry." *Educational Researcher*, vol. 7, no. 2 (February 1978).

Strunk, William, Jr., and E.B. White. *The Elements of Style*. 2nd ed. New York: Macmillan, 1972.

Stufflebeam, Daniel L. *Meta-Evaluation*. Kalamazoo, Mich.: Evaluation Center, Western Michigan University, 1974.

Stufflebeam, Daniel L. "Overview of The Joint Committee's Project on Evaluation Standards." Paper delivered at The Annual Meeting of The American Educational Research Association, New York, N.Y., April 15, 1977.

SUCHMAN, E. A. *Evaluation Research*. New York: Russell Sage Foundation, 1967.

SUDMAN, SEYMOUR. *Applied Sampling*. New York: Academic Press, 1976.

TEY, JOSEPHINE. *The Daughter of Time*. New York: Pocket Books, 1977.

TODD, ALDEN. *Finding Facts Fast: How to Find Out What You Want to Know Immediately*. New York: William Morrow, 1972.

TREMBLAY, MARC-ADÉLARD. "The Key Informant Technique: A Nonethnographic Application." *American Anthropologist*, vol. 59, no. 4 (August 1957), pp. 688–701.

TRIMBLE, JOHN R. *Writing With Style: Conversations on The Art of Writing*. Englewood Cliffs, N.J.: Prentice-Hall 1975.

TURABIAN, KATE L. *Student's Guide For Writing College Papers*. 3rd ed. Chicago, Ill.: Chicago University Press, 1976.

VAN HORN, CARL E. "Studying Policy Implementation," American Political Science Association, 1976.

VAN MANNEN, JOHN. *The Process of Program Evaluation: A Guide For Managers*. Washington, D.C.: National Training and Development Service Press, 1973.

WAX, ROSALIE L. *Doing Fieldwork: Warnings and Advice*. Chicago, Ill.: University of Chicago Press, 1974.

WEBB, EUGENE J.; DONALD F. CAMPBELL; RICHARD D. SCHWARTZ; AND LEE SECHREST. *Unobtrusive Measures: Nonreactive Research in the Social Sciences*. Chicago, Ill.: Rand McNally, 1966.

WEISS, CAROL H., ed. *Evaluating Action Programs: Readings in Social Action and Education*. Boston: Allyn and Bacon, 1972.

WEISS, CAROL H. *Evaluation Research: Methods of Assessing Program Effectiveness*. Englewood Cliffs, N.J.: Prentice-Hall, 1972.

WEISS, CAROL H. "Research for Policy's Sake: The Enlightenment Function of Social Research." *Policy Analysis*, vol. 3, no. 4 (Fall 1977).

WEISS, ROBERT S., AND MARTIN REIN. "The Evaluation of Broad-Aimed Programs: Difficulties in Experimental Design and an Alternative." In *Evaluating Action Programs: Readings in Social Action and Education*, edited by Carol H. Weiss, pp. 236–249. Boston: Allyn and Bacon, 1972.

WELLMAN, FRANCIS L. *The Art of Cross-Examination*. 4th ed. New York: Collier Books, 1936.

WESTLEY, WILLIAM A. "An Analytic-Inductive Model for Evaluation Research." Mimeographed. May 5, 1975.

WHYTE, WILLIAM FOOTE. *Street Corner Society: The Social Structure of An Italian Slum*. 2nd ed. Chicago, Ill.: The University of Chicago Press, 1955.

WILLIAMS, PAUL N. *Investigative Reporting and Editing*. Englewood Cliffs, N.J.: Prentice Hall, 1978.

WILLIAMSON, JOHN B.; DAVID A. KARP; AND JOHN R. DALPHIN. *The Research Craft: An Introduction To Social Science Methods*. Boston: Little, Brown and Company, 1977.

WILLIS, GEORGE, ed. *Qualitative Evaluation: Concepts and Cases in Curriculum Criticism*. Berkeley, Calif.: McCutchan Publishing Corporation, 1978.

WILSON, STEPHEN. "The Use of Ethnographic Techniques in Educational Research." *Review of Educational Research*, vol. 47, no. 2 (Spring 1977), pp. 245–265.

WISEMAN, JACQUELINE P. "The Research Web." *Urban Life and Culture*, vol. 3, no. 3 (October 1974), pp. 317–328.

WOLCOTT, HARRY. "Criteria for an Ethnographic Approach to Research in Schools." *Human Organization*, vol. 34, no. 2 (Summer 1975), pp. 111–127.

WORTHEN, BLAINE R., AND JAMES R. SANDERS. *Educational Evaluation: Theory and Practice*. Belmont, Calif.: Wadsworth Publishing Company, 1973.

YIN, ROBERT K.; KAREN A. HEALD; MARY E. VOGEL; PATRICIA D. FLEISCHAUER; AND BRUCE C. VLADECK. *A Review of Case Studies of Technological Innovations in State and Local Services*. Santa Monica, Calif.: The Rand Corporation, February 1976.

YOUNG, MICHAEL, AND PETER WILLMOTT. *Family and Kinship in East London*. London: Penguin Books, 1962.

ZIEGLER, L. HARMON, AND LLOYD DUVALL. "Freedom of Information Act and Social Science Research," American Educational Research Association Meetings, Toronto, Canada, March 27–31, 1978.

ZINSSER, WILLIAM. *On Writing Well: An Informal Guide to Writing Nonfiction*. New York: Harper and Row, 1976.

Index